LEAD RIGHT FOR YOUR COMPANY'S TYPE

WILLIAM E.
 SCHNEIDER

LEAD RIGHT FOR YOUR COMPANY'S TYPE

HOW TO CONNECT YOUR CULTURE
WITH YOUR CUSTOMER PROMISE

AMACOM
AMERICAN MANAGEMENT ASSOCIATION
New York • Atlanta • Brussels • Chicago • Mexico City • San Francisco
Shanghai • Tokyo • Toronto • Washington, DC

American Management Association: www.amanet.org
This publication is designed to provide accurate and authoritative information in regard to the subject matter covered. It is sold with the understanding that the publisher is not engaged in rendering legal, accounting, or other professional service. If legal advice or other expert assistance is required, the services of a competent professional person should be sought.

Library of Congress Cataloging-in-Publication Data

Names: Schneider, William E., author.
Title: Lead right for your company's type : how to connect your culture with
   your customer promise / William E. Schneider.
Description: New York, NY : AMACOM, [2017] | Includes bibliographical
   references.
Identifiers: LCCN 2017002953 (print) | LCCN 2017018023 (ebook) | ISBN
   9780814438008 (E-book) | ISBN 9780814437995 (hardcover)
Subjects: LCSH: Leadership. | Organizational behavior. | Corporate culture. |
   Customer relations.
Classification: LCC HD57.7 (ebook) | LCC HD57.7 .S35626 2017 (print) | DDC
   658.4/092--dc23
LC record available at https://lccn.loc.gov/2017002953

About AMA
American Management Association (www.amanet.org) is a world leader in talent development, advancing the skills of individuals to drive business success. Our mission is to support the goals of individuals and organizations through a complete range of products and services, including classroom and virtual seminars, webcasts, webinars, podcasts, conferences, corporate and government solutions, business books, and research. AMA's approach to improving performance combines experiential learning—learning through doing—with opportunities for ongoing professional growth at every step of one's career journey.

10 9 8 7 6 5 4 3 2 1

"An organization is a human, a social, indeed a moral phenomenon."

—PETER DRUCKER
Quoted in Micklethwait, J., and Wooldridge, A., *The Witch Doctors*

"Companies are communities. There's a spirit of working together. Companies are not a place where a few people allow themselves to be singled out as solely responsible for success."

—HENRY MINTZBERG,
Quoted in Moore, K., "Transcript: Why a good boss needs to focus on community." *Globe & Mail*

"Understanding human organizations as living systems is one of the critical challenges of our time."

—FRITJOF CAPRA, *The Hidden Connections*

"The visible world is the invisible energy of organization."

—HEINZ PAGELS, Physicist, *The Cosmic Code*

"All things are connected. Whatever befalls the earth, befalls the sons of the earth."   —Attributed to CHIEF SEATTLE, 1854

"If a thing is not good for the hive, it is not good for the bee."

—MARCUS AURELIUS, *Meditations*

"Leadership is the process of creating an environment in which people become empowered."

—GERALD WEINBERG, *Becoming a Technical Leader:*
An Organic Problem-Solving Approach

"The major problems of the world are the result of the difference between the way nature works and the way people think."

—GREGORY BATESON

"The business of business is people. Yesterday, today, and forever."

—HERB KELLEHER

"A human being is part of the whole, called by us *the Universe*, a part limited by time and space. He experiences himself, his thoughts and feelings, as something separate from the rest—a kind of optical delusion of consciousness. This delusion is a prison. . . . Our task must be to free ourselves by widening our circle of compassion to embrace all living creatures and the whole of nature in its beauty."

—ALBERT EINSTEIN, Quoted in Fleurmach.com

ACKNOWLEDGMENTS

This book has been long in the making. Soon after I wrote my first book on organizational culture, I set out on a path to link culture to customer promise and leadership. My reasoning was that, without that linkage, information on culture would be helpful, but not impactful enough. My view then (and now) is that customer promise, culture, and leadership must be addressed together and that, until such is done, it is difficult to make a substantive and lasting contribution to the success of any enterprise. I hope that this book goes a long way toward making that contribution for leaders. But, I could not, and did not, get to this stage alone.

Which leads me to all those people to whom I owe a great deal of gratitude.

Nick Colarelli started me down the path of looking at organizations as systems and has been a guiding force in my professional life for the last 39 years. Rich Fortin was a wise and thoughtful colleague who helped me crystallize my thinking about connecting customers, employees, and leaders. Tom Rand helped me immeasurably with assessment system design. Kyle Davis has effectively contributed much to the design, scoring, and presentation of the results of all of our assessments. Michael Ihlenburg has greatly helped us build online platforms for our assessments and websites. Rad Eanes continues to this day to be a great friend and colleague who always provides me with valuable insights and advice.

All of our 261 colleagues in our network of consultants have helped advance the concepts and methods in this book by bringing us in to work with them and their clients. Our colleagues at Spencer, Shenk, and Capers; TAP Resource Development Group; Lee Hecht Harrison; Insperity; PA Consulting Group; and Hedron Consulting Group have helped our firm progress and refine the framework and methodology in this book. I am particularly grateful to Sharon Dye, Brad Spencer, Tom Shenk, Dan Collett, Susan Peirce, Richard Gerstberger, Kevin Purcell, Geoffrey Moore, Peter Moore, Dan Guenther, Arnold Sykes, and Madeline McGill for their long-standing collaboration with us over many years.

Our clients over the years are too many to name here. They have helped us refine and continually develop our thinking and approach. We would not be where we are today without them. I want to give special thanks to Sean Burke, Jana Burke, John Williams, Kay Norton, Robbyn Wacker, Gloria Reynolds, Wolf Hengst, Dan Henig, Herb Schulze, Sam King, Bob Dalton, Mike Smith, Jana Edwards, and Rick Poppe.

Mike Snell, my literary agent, has encouraged me since we first met in mid-2015. His no-nonsense thinking, long years of experience in the publishing business, and sound advice have made a huge difference in getting this book to market.

I can't praise Libby Koponen, my editor, enough. She is superb at her craft, has a blend of writing expertise and knowledge of what works for readers, and tons of integrity. She grasped my concepts immediately and made the book readable and helped me make the concepts accessible and easily understood. She is also a great consultant!

Stephen S. Power, senior editor at AMACOM, has been in my corner every step of the way. He has been a strong supporter of this book within AMACOM. Also thanks to Tim Burgard, senior editor at AMACOM, for his guidance in getting the manuscript ready for production.

My wife, Kristine, deserves a medal for putting up with me in the long process of bringing this book to press. She has been a strong supporter of me and my work, a valuable sounding board, and a caring companion. Finally, I want to thank my children, Bill, Michael, Greg, and Mary for their continuous support and encouragement—even as the timeline for completing the book stretched out further than anticipated.

CONTENTS

FOREWORD

I first met Bill Schneider when he was admitted to St. Louis University's psychology program as a graduate student. I was a member of the graduate faculty at that time. It was my good fortune that he selected me as his advisor. I soon discovered that he was a cut above his fellow students in his capacity for abstract thinking. He perceived patterns and relationships that were indiscernible to others. It was impressive to watch him struggle to find words and metaphors to make the indiscernible communicable to the rest of us. Early on he developed an interest in systems theory and became a voracious student of anything related to it. His reading reinforced his tendency to look beyond the obvious, to probe more deeply, and to search for the "connectedness of things." As a graduate student he honed this interest and inclination into a mental discipline that has served him well throughout his career.

After I left the University, Bill joined me as a colleague in my consulting firm. We worked together on organizational development projects for several years and had the opportunity to gain experience with a number of different types of organizations. Bill's interests at that time were focused on organizational culture and leadership. He later moved on to a number of larger human resource consulting firms. Our friendship remained intact but our paths diverged. We continued to communicate with each other over these years, recommending books to each other, sharing experiences in working with our respective clients, and engaging in discussions about organizational theory and the critical role of leadership. During these intervening years he continued to pursue his interest in system theory and developed the core concepts contained in this book: organizations as living systems—self organizing, homeostatic and evolving networks; the four distinct types of organizations; the inextricable linkage of customer purpose, culture and leadership; the attention and decision-making axis, etc. He continued to identify the linkages among them and elaborate on the impact of their misalignment and disconnection. Eventually Bill established his own firm. There he created an on-going research program that was fully integrated with the firm's practice model. This combination enabled him to continue to test, refine and further develop the body of work that is the content of this book.

This book represents a career-long process of developing, testing and communication of ideas used with organizational leaders that eventuated in a comprehensive, integrated, systemic model with tools that make it useful and practical for executives. Why do leaders need to read this book?

First, it is written for "doers." Its style is clear, lucid and business-like. It can be read in a short amount of time. It takes complex ideas and relationships and presents them with a direct line of sight to their practical use.

Secondly, it is a serious book. It is not a "Leader of the Month" book, nor is it a "Ten Best Practices Manual" delivered in "snackbite" style. It is a book by a brilliant scholar-practitioner who has spent his career understanding what current science has to say about the real world we live in and its implications for human organizations and living systems. It is a complex meta-analysis of human organizations, and yet it is readable and practical. Based on hard science, the concepts it presents are fundamental and will endure.

Thirdly, it is an important leadership tool. Leadership requires judgement calls—often among competing options that are equally attractive for different reasons. What Bill has produced for leaders is a framework for developing and maintaining coherence in their organizations as they make those judgment calls. The frameworks, principles, and tools described here can be used for:

Clarifying the identity of the business and testing decisions for coherence with that identity.

Reducing conflict arising from processes and expectations that cut across each other.

Problem solving—discovering where and how enterprise systems are not functioning in the service of the whole.

Vetting proposed strategic and operational solutions.

Enabling employees to understand and take pride in their contribution.

Providing practical guidelines for application of the content and for vetting content from other sources.

I treasure my forty year relationship with Bill, whom I have come to know not only as a brilliant and dedicated professional, but also as kind and caring person of the highest integrity. It is my hope that you will come to appreciate his work as I have.

Nick J. Colarelli, Ph.D.

INTRODUCTION

Your Enterprise Is a Living People System

M icrosoft dominated its market in 1998. The hugely successful technology enterprise's software operating systems ran on 86.3 percent of all the personal computers in the United States. Then something happened to bring the giant to its knees: The technology group stopped reporting directly to Bill Gates and began focusing on reporting profits and losses. Instead of developing new and more effective technology for consumers, the company insisted that the technology group only propose ideas that could turn a quick profit. In three short years Microsoft lost more than half its value.

Ron Johnson, successful senior VP of retail operations at Apple, left to take over the helm at J. C. Penney in 2011. He immediately changed J. C. Penney's practice of leadership, power, and compensation. He did what he had done so successfully at Apple—but two years later, J. C. Penney's sales had plunged 25 percent and he was asked to leave.

Neither Bill Gates nor Ron Johnson understood why they ran into trouble.

Microsoft slid because Gates implemented the leadership, power, and compensation practices of a predictable and dependable enterprise in a best-in-class enterprise. Johnson did the opposite. He adopted the leadership, power, and compensation practices of a best-in-class enterprise in a predictable and dependable enterprise. The conflicting approaches pulled each company apart. Performance plummeted.

All enterprises fall into one of four basic types, as shown in Figure i-1.

Each has corresponding types of customer promise, culture, and leadership. To succeed, enterprises need to use the right kinds of practice for their type and connect them the right way. When one type of enterprise uses the practices of a different type—as Microsoft and J. C. Penney did—the disconnections pull the enterprise apart.

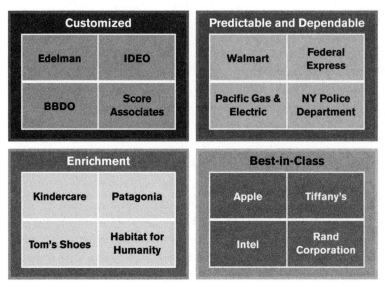

Figure i-1. The Four Living Enterprises

The Science of Living Systems

Surprisingly, this can be explained scientifically. For the last fifty years, scientists have been studying the nature and behavior of all living systems. They have concluded that all living systems are networks of dynamic and properly ordered connections—each network is the *reality* of that particular living system. "Network" means an arrangement, a pattern. "Dynamic" means alive, evolving, creating, growing, ever-developing. "Connections" means interdependencies or links. Even more surprisingly, each kind of system—from subatomic particles to biological cells to supernovas—has its own kind of network and can be divided into distinct types.

The science of living systems encompasses an amazing set of scientific disciplines: subatomic physics, physics, biochemistry, molecular biology, chemistry, biology, anatomy, physiology, information theory, cognitive theory, psychology, anthropology, sociology, ecology, cosmology, and astrophysics (among others). What has emerged from the research is that all living systems share distinctive characteristics. Each system is a whole, and it is not reducible to its components. Its distinctive nature derives from the *dynamic relationships* of its parts. It is the *connectivity* of the parts that establishes the *reality* of every living system. Secondly, each living system is self-organizing, self-stabilizing, and maintains a homeostasis (it stays in balance). Continuous feedback allows these processes to occur. Thirdly, each evolves and grows, which also requires continuous feedback. Finally, each is both a whole in its own right and simultaneously an integral part of a larger system.

Every living system is based on interdependence. Its living elements are interwoven. The viability ("success") of every living system depends on the preservation of this interdependence. The living system's *connections* underpin its ability to live and its capacity to operate and sustain itself. Different kinds of living systems have their own distinct network or pattern of connections. Every living organism continually renews itself while maintaining its overall identity, or pattern of organization. At a biological level, our pancreas replaces most of its cells every twenty-four hours, the cells of our stomach lining are reproduced every three days, our white blood cells are renewed in ten days, and 98 percent of the protein in our brain is turned over in less than one month. Every living system also is continually adapting, learning, and developing.

I wrote this book to convince you that profit and nonprofit enterprises are living people systems and that embracing this belief (and its implications) will significantly change your leadership for the better. Customers, employees, and leaders are not commodities, and they are not separate from one another. They are different, but they are not separate. If you take away any one of the three—customers, employees, or leaders— you don't have an enterprise! Enterprises are started by people, led by people, operated by people, improved by people, perpetuated by people, dissolved by people. People create and provide value for people. People are the life of your enterprise. Customers, employees, and leaders are all that is alive in an enterprise, and they are inextricably and vitally woven together. The promise that you make to your customer, your culture of employees, and your leadership approach are immutably intertwined.

Customer Promise, Culture, and Leadership

When we promise a product or service to customers, we form an immediate interdependence with them. They are now "depending upon" us to deliver on our promise. Our promise connects them with our living people system. They are not "outside" our enterprise. Every enterprise exists to deliver on its promise to its customers. The four fundamental enterprises discussed in this book are each named by their customer promise—predictable and dependable, enrichment, best-in-class, and customized. Everything starts with your customer promise. Customer promise determines your culture and leadership approach. There is no one right culture or leadership approach. One size does not fit all.

Culture means how we hire, structure, deploy, compensate, and develop our employees to deliver on our customer promise. It establishes and underpins, among other factors, structure, membership criteria, conditions for judging effective performance, communication patterns, expectations and priorities, the nature of reward and compensation, the nature and use of power, decision-making practices, and teaming practices. It is about our community of employees. It is about *how* we do things in order to succeed. It is all about implementation. Over time, if we are more and more successful, culture becomes equivalent to our identity (e.g., the GE way, the Disney way, the Apple way). The more successful our enterprise is, the stronger our culture becomes. Culture is *not* a compilation of individual people's values. Culture is essentially formed by what it takes for your people to fully deliver on your enterprise's customer promise. It is driven by the nature of your business and what it takes for you to succeed in your marketplace.

Leadership means to set a direction for your enterprise based on customer promise, to mobilize commitment, and to build enterprise capability. It is where greater power exists in order to influence events within the enterprise. Leadership includes people who lack observable rank or title. The more versatile the leader, the more effective he or she is. Versatile leaders understand their core approach to leadership and adapt that approach to the strategic and cultural requirements inherent in their type of enterprise. They create conditions for their whole enterprise to fully deliver on its customer promise. At the end of the day, leadership is about creating unity and empowering people to live up to the enterprise's customer promise.

People Problems

I have been working with leaders in all walks of life, profit and nonprofit, for more than thirty-five years now and have come to appreciate how hard leadership can be. It is complex and high-pressured work. And, in my experience with more than 4,000 leaders, the most difficult aspect of it is leading people.

So it's not surprising that most leadership books focus on people-related issues. Figure i-2 is a beginning list of people issues.

■ Persistent internal conflicts	■ Reluctance to raise issues or concerns
■ Distrust	■ Considerable blaming of one another
■ Employee disengagement	■ Agreements reached, but lack follow through
■ Low level of cooperation, coordination	
■ Functional silos	■ Excessive committees and unnecessary meetings
■ Low morale	
■ Implementation problems	■ Presence of factions, in-groups, out-groups
■ Over-prevalence of self-preservation	■ Difficulty getting people to team with one another
■ Workflow bottlenecks	
■ Confusion about responsibility	■ Low sense of urgency
■ Customers taken for granted	■ Frequent hiring mistakes
■ Ineffective performance management	■ People avoid conflict
■ Leaders hoarding power	■ High level of frustration
■ People getting into power battles	■ Frequent leadership changes
■ Turf battles	■ High degree of manipulation
■ High level of employee and/or leader turnover	■ People reluctant to take on new or additional responsibilities
■ Duplication of work	■ Complaints about promotion decisions
■ Leaders sending contradictory messages	■ Difficulty instituting/executing change
■ Communication breakdowns	■ People afraid to take risks; too much playing it safe
■ Too much politicking	
■ Low level of accountability	■ People bad-mouth one another
■ People refuse to take responsibility for mistakes	■ Low level of productivity
	■ People feel demoralized
■ People keep "passing the buck" to someone else	■ People detached from enterprise
	■ Going through the motions
■ Employees afraid to give leaders bad news	■ Lack of commitment
	■ People fatigued/overworked
■ People punished for giving leaders bad news	■ High level of fear
■ Customers getting mixed messages	

Figure i-2. People Issues

If you *step back* and look at all of these problems over the years, two interesting patterns show up. One, they keep reappearing, year in and year out. Two, they are typically addressed one or two at a time.

If you *drill down*, however, an even more interesting pattern shows up. All these problems have to do with people separating from one another: in silos, by disengaging, by thinking they understand when they don't. When leaders believe everybody is clear about the direction of their enterprise, but employees perform in a way that doesn't fit that direction, leaders and employees are separated. When people blame one another for mistakes, they create separation. These separations, or disconnections, involve customers, employees, and leaders, and separations between any one set (e.g., leaders and employees) impact all three.

These disconnections keep reappearing because they are *symptoms* of a deeper problem—hidden system disconnections. These are the root cause of people issues. The four enterprises described in this book are four fundamentally different living people systems. Each of the four has its own particular set of properly ordered connections, as living systems research would put it. The "properly ordered" connections for each are described in Chapters 2–5. Each approaches its customers differently, each practices fifteen culture drivers differently, and each practices three leadership drivers differently.

Customers, employees, and leaders are an interdependent network. When you do something to interfere with this interdependence, you cause disconnections and prompt the appearance of symptoms. If you try to implement consensus decision-making in a best-in-class enterprise or try to practice "steward" leadership in a predictable and dependable enterprise, you create contradictions and crosscurrents. You take your enterprise off course and cause your employees to lose respect for you. Because these separations are hidden, the symptoms persist or subside and then reappear.

The more your customers, employees, and leaders are properly connected for your kind of enterprise, the more successful you will be. The less they are properly connected, the more "people issues" you will have and the less successful you will be.

This book will change how you think about leadership and how you practice it. It will give you a way to unite your people and get them working together. It will help you get to the root causes of your "people problems" and what to do about them. If your enterprise is stuck, it will give you a way to change that and free up you and your people. It will bring to light hidden forces that have been holding your enterprise back. It will infuse positive energy into your enterprise. It will give you a step-by-step way to significantly increase the success of your enterprise.

Section I describes the four living enterprises and the system-centric mindset. Chapter 1 shows you how to determine your enterprise type and includes a table of culture and leadership drivers and how each type should practice them. One CEO of a major retailer keeps this table on the wall of his office. Chapters 2–5 thoroughly describe the four enterprise types in terms of their customer promise, showing how to practice the culture and leadership drivers correctly for each type. Chapter 6 shows how to adopt a system-centric mindset and what happens when you do. Section II gives you a proven methodology for connecting your customer promise, culture, and leadership.

Chapters 7–11 present a systematic framework and process for:

- Finding your focus
- Discovering the hidden disconnections that are separating your people and weakening your enterprise
- Practicing the culture and leadership drivers in the right ways for your enterprise type
- Staying in balance and preventing your strengths from becoming weaknesses
- Continuing to adapt

The Appendix describes the validated assessments that we have developed to help our clients diagnose their own enterprises and implement development programs.

By the end of the book, you will not only understand how to solve people problems—you will have learned how to prevent future problems and keep your enterprise on the path to success.

THE FOUR LIVING ENTERPRISES

1

THE FOUR LIVING ENTERPRISES
Determining Your Organization's Type

➤ ➤ ➤

John Garner, VP Operations for an oil drilling company, was chatting with his drilling supervisor, Frank. Frank mentioned that he had hired a sensitivity consultant to work with his tool-pushers, those who guide the oil drill into the ground. John, curious, asked if he could attend one of the sessions.

The tool-pushers sat in a circle while the consultant asked them each to tell how they felt about the others; obviously uncomfortable, the men said as little as they could. This went on for an hour. Try as he might, John could see no earthly reason for any of it. He knew that when people are operating complicated machinery like drilling rigs, their attention needs to be totally focused on what they are doing, not people's feelings. If their attention wanders from the drill even for an instant, they put themselves and others at risk. So after the meeting, John spoke to Frank. "What were you thinking?" John said, and told Frank to fire the consultant.

Frank was shocked. A friend had recommended the training, which had really helped the employees at a PR firm get along better. But it was worse than useless in an oilfield—and potentially dangerous.

Ideas like this come out of left field all the time due to the one-size-fits-all mentality that dominates too much business thinking today. That approach assumes that what works in one enterprise will work in another. Although it is propounded by many, many consultants and books, this approach does not work.

If you don't know already which type of enterprise yours is, you will by the end of this chapter. This chapter will:

- Describe the four fundamental kinds of enterprises
- Show how the four kinds of enterprises focus attention and make decisions
- Tell you how to determine which is yours

The Four Types of Enterprises

What an enterprise promises its customers determines its type. Customer promise is an enterprise's magnetic north—it guides enterprises to the right culture and leadership practices. These practices are completely different in each of the four enterprise types. Taking the cultural and leadership practices of one type of enterprise and trying to force them on another type pulls an enterprise apart.

But this is just what many business books advise leaders to do. I searched "consensus decision-making" on Amazon books in January 2017 and came up with 153 results. Each of these 153 books is claiming that consensus decision-making is right for every enterprise. But consensus decision-making works only in a customized enterprise—there, decisions should be based on the collective judgments of the team. For example, an architect and client need to make many decisions together to come up with a house that suits the customer. This kind of decision-making would be disastrous at a predictable and dependable enterprise like a utility company or NASA, where decisions often need to be made very quickly and must be based on facts, data, and established procedures.

The customized enterprise promises a unique tailored solution to each customer. It must partner closely with each customer and discuss decisions in detail, which takes highly collaborative leadership and cultural practices. For example, Ogilvy & Mather provides a customized PR campaign for customers. Each customer gets its own carefully built team of people. Leadership is participative and helps team members work together and deliver on the company's customer promise. The customer is always a member of the team.

The predictable and dependable enterprise promises customers reliability, safety, security, or, sometimes, commodities. For example, predictable and dependable enterprises like Pacific Gas & Electric (PG&E) keep tight control with highly structured leadership and cultural practices; consistent, efficient operations; and clear, detailed policies and procedures. Decisions depend on facts and data. Directive, authoritative leadership focuses on attaining operational goals and adhering to role requirements.

The best-in-class enterprise promises superior products and/or services. Best-in-class enterprises like Apple need the most expert people they can find to imagine and innovate products and services. Leaders and cultural practices focus on excellence. Expertise remains center stage. Decisions are based on facts and hard data. This enterprise must constantly innovate, so leaders identify challenges and then challenge others to be the best that they can be. People follow leaders in this enterprise because they believe in being the best.

The enrichment enterprise aims to help people fulfill their potential, have a healthier life, and realize higher-level purposes. For example, Habitat for Humanity helps house less-fortunate people. It keeps its values center stage and focuses on applying them for the betterment of others. Leadership and cultural practices empower customers and employees. Decision-making depends on values, and decisions in this enterprise type are highly subjective. Leaders energize others, continually striving to realize the potential in employees and customers. Enrichment enterprises grow organically.

Leadership, Empowerment, and Culture in the Four Enterprise Types

Leadership is about empowerment—creating the conditions for employees, managers, and fellow leaders to deliver on the enterprise's customer promise. But different types of enterprises must use empowerment in different ways. For example, an electric utility can't empower employees to "follow what they believe in"—that would create chaos and danger. A PR firm has to include the customer on the team and empower the team to consensually come to its best judgment about what the customer's PR campaign should look like.

Culture is about implementation and identity. Culture means how we hire, structure, deploy, compensate, and develop our employees to deliver on our customer promise. Culture is essentially formed by what it takes for your people to fully deliver on your enterprise's customer promise. It is driven by the nature of your business and what it takes for you to succeed in your marketplace.

In short, the four enterprise types are four different worlds and can't practice empowerment or culture the same way. What drives the culture and leadership of the four enterprise types is different, depending upon the kind of customer promise they have. These drivers and how they should be practiced in each type of enterprise are all discussed in detail in the next four chapters, but Figures 1-1a through 1-1c and Figure 1-2 list them all and summarize each type's basic approach to them. Control culture aligns to predictable and dependable type organizations; collaboration to customized organizations; competence to best-in-class and cultivation aligns to enrichment organizations.

Core Culture	Compensation	Nature and Use of Power	Decision Making	Managing Change	Managing Performance
Control	Tie to operational goal attainment	Role/ Operations	Impersonal Operational system performance	Anticipate it and plan for it	Ensure that performance accomplishes operational system goals
Collaboration	Tie to collective accomplishment and to team performance	Knowledgeable Relationship	Personal Consensus	Team calls for change	Performance accomplishes unique customer goals
Competence	Tie to outstanding, unique, one-of-a-kind, proven performance	Expertise	Impersonal Expertise-based	Achievement goals drive change	Performance achieves conceptual goals
Cultivation	Tie to the extent to which espoused values are realized	Belief/Will	Personal Values-based	Embrace; assume change	Performance operationalizes values-centered goals

Figure 1-1a. Summary of Culture Drivers

Core Culture	Managing Innovation	Managing Conflict	Nature of Work	Role of Employee	Organizational Structure
Control	Structure process for coming up with new ideas	Carefully review the evidence by various levels of management	Functionalist emphasis	Adhere to role requirements	Hierarchy
Collaboration	Continually brainstorm with selves and customers	Utilize fully to come up with what will work best for each customer	Generalist emphasis	Actively participate as team member	Group, cluster
Competence	Ensure that innovative, leading-edge thinking is constant	Treat as central to enterprise's ability to deliver best-in-class products/services	Specialist emphasis	Be the best, be an expert	Matrix, adhocracy
Cultivation	Invite people to contribute as many ideas as they believe will help	Utilize it as an opportunity to do more to realize our values	Functionalist, generalist, specialist	Work to realize the values of the enterprise	Wheel-like, circular, lattice

Figure 1-1b. Summary of Culture Drivers

Core Culture	Teaming	Info Technology	Selection (Hiring)	People Development	Promotion
Control	Cross-functional	Improve operational efficiency	Determined by fit with functional requirements	Emphasis on formal, structured training	Based on consistent performance within a function
Collaboration	Win-win. Very diverse team members	Help enterprise stay in continual contact with one another and customer	Determined by fit with team and kind of customer	Emphasis on on-the-job training	Based on extent to which customers are well-served
Competence	Project-oriented Members are carefully-chosen experts. Win-lose	Help enterprise get the best and latest information as quickly as possible	Determined by fit with unique specialist expertise required	Emphasis on development of specialist expertise	Based on consistent demonstration of technical or special expertise

Figure 1-1c. Summary of Culture Drivers

(cont'd. on next page)

(cont'd. from previous page)

Core Culture	Teaming	Info Technology	Selection (Hiring)	People Development	Promotion
Cultivation	Teams take all kinds of different shapes Members join teams to make a contribution	Utilize to handle the basics so enterprise can attend to what matters most	Determined by fit with enterprise beliefs and values	Emphasis on improving realization of enterprise's values	Based on demonstration of living up to the values and purpose of the enterprise

Figure 1-1c. Summary of Culture Drivers

Core Leadership Approach	Set Direction	Mobilize Commitment	Build Organizational Capability
Directive	Establish operational goals and objectives	Clarify how function, roles, and people contribute to operational goal attainment	Build operational systems
Participative	Stay close to each customer Direction is unique to each customer	Capitalize on the power of relationships	Ensure that the customer is closely involved in every key decision
Standard Setter	Communicate unique and distinctive concepts that need to be achieved	Recognize outstanding achievements	Establish processes for systematically measuring hypothesized vs. actual
Charismatic	Capture and communicate essential values to be realized	Foster dedication	Ensure that resources are centered on realizing values

Figure 1-2. Summary of Leadership

Attention and Decision-Making

What an organization pays attention to and how it makes decisions drive the delivery of its customer promise. Each enterprise type is a unique blend of where it puts its attention and how it makes decisions. In Figure

1-3, the vertical axis shows what an enterprise primarily pays attention to. The horizontal axis shows how an enterprise primarily makes decisions.

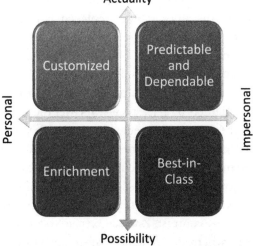

Figure 1-3. Attention and Decision-Making

The attention axis has *Actuality* at one end and *Possibility* at the other; the decision-making axis has *Impersonal* at one end and *Personal* at the other. Customized enterprises and predictable and dependable enterprises are actuality enterprises. Enrichment enterprises and best-in-class enterprises are possibility enterprises. Customized and enrichment are personal enterprises. Predictable and dependable and best-in-class are impersonal enterprises.

Each enterprise is a unique mix of one attention element and one decision-making element. Customized is an actuality-personal enterprise; predictable and dependable is actuality-impersonal; enrichment is possibility-personal; and best-in-class is possibility-impersonal. An enterprise's unique mix of attention and decision-making can include elements from other types. For example, predictable and dependable and best-in-class enterprises both make decisions based on facts and hard data; this means that both make decisions *primarily* by relying on facts and hard data. It does not mean that they never consider personal matters when they make decisions. Every enterprise's main tendencies are like right- and left-handedness in people: One hand dominates, but we use both hands. Similarly, one way of making decisions dominates an enterprise, but it will use other ways at times.

Attention

John (Skip) Coleman, deputy chief of fire prevention, Toledo (Ohio) Department of Fire and Rescue, once said that of all the advances in firefighting apparatus since motors replaced horses he considered "positive-pressure self-contained breathing apparatus [SCBA] to be the greatest. That along with National Fire Protection Association [NFPA] 1500 and mandatory mask policies developed by the NFPA and OSHA [Occupational Safety and Health Administration] have extended the life expectancy of firefighters by at least ten years over those who fought fires without them." The SCBA was invented by Zodiac Oxygen Systems U.S.

The Toledo Department of Fire and Rescue and Zodiac Oxygen Systems are both in the firefighting business, but what each pays attention to couldn't be more different. Toledo Department of Fire and Rescue firefighters deal with the immediate present: When the bell rings, they spring into action. By contrast, Zodiac Oxygen Systems' workers spend their time on what will make firefighters safe in the future. They envision, design, test, and experiment with new kinds of equipment to make firefighters safer.

At the most fundamental level, every enterprise focuses either on the actual or the possible. Actuality has to do with what is; possibility has to do what might be. The Toledo Department of Fire and Rescue is an actuality enterprise and Zodiac Oxygen Systems is a possibility enterprise.

An actuality enterprise focuses on:

- Concrete, tangible reality
- Immediate customer demand
- Actual experience/actual occurrence

A possibility enterprise focuses on:

- Imagined alternatives
- What might occur in the future
- Innovations/creative options
- Theoretical concepts or frameworks
- Ideals/beliefs

The actuality enterprise lives in immediate experience and reality. The possibility enterprise lives in anticipation and possibility.

Compare our enterprise pairs. The actuality enterprises—customized and predictable and dependable—focus on getting today's job done. A public relations firm offers a customized solution for each customer that increases marketplace exposure—in its current marketplace. It builds a PR campaign that fits who the customer actually is and what her company actually does, today. The customer implements the PR campaign as soon as it is ready. Similarly, a predictable and dependable enterprise provides a product or service today: A fire needs to be put out immediately, emergency room patients have to be treated ASAP, an electric utility has to provide predictable and dependable electricity 24/7.

By contrast, enrichment and best-in-class enterprises, the possibility enterprises, focus on goals that take time to reach—educating children, or creating one-of-a-kind products or services that may take years to design and develop. The next, distinctive smartphone may take ten years to imagine, design, build, and test before it is actually available for sale. Helping children to fulfill their potential is a future-focused endeavor. A scientific theory may take fifty years to be proven or disproven. Inspiration and imagined alternatives fuel these enterprises. Workers engage in explorations that stretch far beyond present reality. For enrichment and best-in-class enterprises, life lies beyond the horizon.

To sum up: Customized and predictable and dependable focus on present needs. Enrichment and best-in-class enterprises focus on future goals.

Decision-Making

Market Point describes itself as a "storytelling firm working with new companies to build engaging brands that inspire." It "partners with" clients and helps them develop "their own stories that inspire and reach into audience's hearts and minds. . . . We build emotional, intuitive and visceral connections. We collaborate closely with you and work step by step with you to build a PR campaign."

TrendKite's software helps PR agencies build a timely, highly accurate picture of their media coverage. TrendKite promises "deep domain expertise and thorough understanding of the complex PR landscape. Together we are focused on the problems around PR analytics and reporting. We've felt your pain. To relieve it, we are bringing to bear the latest in big data analytics technology and presenting it elegantly."

Market Point and TrendKite are both in the public relations business but make decisions totally differently. Market Point and each customer decide together. They brainstorm ideas, experiment, and interpret the marketplace together. TrendKite bases all of its decision-making on hard data, analytics, dashboards, and quantitative formulas. The essence of its business is to provide verifiable information.

When making decisions, every enterprise emphasizes either impersonal data-based analysis or personal judgment-making. Personal decision-making relies on individuals' and groups' own subjective, values-based judgments. Impersonal decision-making relies on data and detached reasoning. The process is different in each.

The decision process in personal enterprises is:

- People coming to a judgment
- Organic/evolutionary/dynamic
- Participative
- Subjective
- Open-ended
- Emotional

The decision process in impersonal enterprises is:

- Detached reasoning
- Fact and data based
- System, policy, and procedure oriented
- Objective
- Formula oriented
- Law oriented
- Emotionless

A personal process enterprise relies on the minds and hearts of people— their values, beliefs, and mutually arrived-at judgments—to make decisions. An impersonal process enterprise relies on systems, data, facts, formulas, and methods to make decisions.

Customized and enrichment enterprises are personal decision-making enterprises. Decisions in a customized enterprise are made by consensus, and customers are closely involved. Decisions in an enrichment enterprise are made according to values. These two enterprise types are focused on forming judgments and trust their people to make them. Decision-making is quite subjective; mistakes are par for the course. The judgment and wisdom of people carries the enterprise forward.

For example, a PR firm typically operates with teams of very diverse people, puts the customer on the team, and brainstorms and pushes for consensus. An enrichment enterprise centers its decision-making on its values and the extent to which those values are realized. It is belief-driven.

An enterprise that provides physical therapy to patients needs to know how well the patient *feels*. A nonprofit enterprise that finds and provides foster parents relies upon personal judgment to decide whether or not particular foster parents are benefiting the child under their care.

Predictable and dependable and best-in-class enterprises make decisions by prescribing operational systems, formulas, and methods for people to follow. They provide people with ways to get and keep control, emphasizing precedents and requiring objectivity and order. People decide based on facts and hard data, using established policies and procedures.

For example, decisions in a nuclear power plant are based on hard data, gauges, and fact-based reports. Police need reliable information and data to catch lawbreakers. Low-margin grocery stores require constant tracking of inventory, product placement, and customer buying patterns. Low-price retail operations that sell necessities need the same.

A best-in-class enterprise establishes achievement goals and deploys people to reach them. It sets standards and challenges people to surpass them. People often use the scientific method, which relies on formal logic and emphasizes an empirical approach. A scientific research firm emphasizes hypotheses and then uses the scientific method to test them. A high-tech firm building sophisticated software bases decisions on tests to ensure that the software actually does what it promises. A consulting firm that offers a proprietary methodology for determining where exactly a customer derives its greatest return on investment has to develop a formula and then be able to prove that it works. These enterprises must rely on externally verifiable data to succeed.

Opposite Enterprise Pairs

Enterprises on the diagonal to one another in Figure 1-3 are opposites. Customized (actuality-personal) enterprises contrast most sharply with best-in-class (possibility-impersonal) enterprises; predictable and dependable (actuality-impersonal) contrast with enrichment (possibility-personal). Interestingly, knowing about these opposite enterprise pairs helps you understand and predict more about each enterprise.

For example, you can predict that a best-in-class enterprise will struggle with teaming by knowing that its opposite, a customized enterprise, relies on teams. Conversely, you can predict that a customized enterprise will have trouble using expertise by knowing that its opposite, a best-in-class enterprise, relies on expertise. Just picture a Ph.D. scientist expounding about relativity to a PR firm's clients!

Similarly, customized enterprises can get very close to customers; best-in-class enterprises can get lost in ideas and pay too little attention to customers. A predictable and dependable enterprise tends to take its customers for granted (e.g., describes them as "ratepayers"); an enrichment enterprise tends to have trouble scaling its business and balancing its books.

An enrichment enterprise may tend to have too much mission and not enough margin; put another way, it has a hard time controlling operations. It's preoccupied by its intention—benefiting others and helping them have a better life. Adhering to a budget often contravenes its organic, evolutionary growth. A predictable and dependable enterprise tends to take its people for granted and not train them enough. It has a hard time empowering employees, which is a hallmark of an enrichment enterprise. An enrichment enterprise fully embraces change; a predictable and dependable enterprise has huge difficulty with it, trying to anticipate change and stop it from happening.

A customized enterprise meets too much; a best-in-class enterprise doesn't meet enough. A predictable and dependable enterprise tends to ignore the purpose and value of what it is doing; an enrichment enterprise emphasizes both too much and struggles with how to build a more systematic way to accomplish its goals.

How to Determine Your Enterprise Type

By now, you may know your enterprise type; if not, this last section will help you learn what it is. Before we begin, there is one caveat: Your enterprise may consist of many enterprise types because it has different customer promises. This happens roughly 20 percent of the time. If this is the case, restructure your enterprise into as many separate and singularly focused strategic business units or lines of businesses as you have customer promises. Not doing so will embed a myriad of cross-purpose behaviors that will impede each enterprise.

If you are already a holding company, like General Electric (GE), apply the information in this section to each separate strategic business unit or line of business under your over-arching umbrella.

When determining your enterprise type, base your thinking on your core enterprise. "Core" means everything required to deliver on your customer promise. A simple way to find the core of your enterprise is to ask what your enterprise needs to stay in business. If you can outsource it, then it is not part of your core; it is support to the core. A support unit itself can be a "sub-enterprise" and be any one of the four customer-culture-leadership networks. The core is the support unit's customer.

Your customer promise determines your type. Because words—including "customer promise"—could mean different things to different people, when trying to determine this clearly, look at how you actually interact with your customers. Focus on how you behave with your customers to learn your type. For example, ask yourself: What exact behaviors do we actually exhibit when we deliver on our customer promise? What exactly is our customer buying?

In our experience, many leaders believe that their enterprise is a mixture of two, three, or even all four of the enterprises discussed in this book. When we started with Synergis Education, the company's leaders believed that their enterprise was both a customized enterprise and a best-in-class enterprise. They had their own definition of each. But, when we simply asked them to describe exactly what the enterprise does (what exact actions it takes and in what sequence), it became crystal clear that they were in the best-in-class business. They designed software—the best of its kind!—their customers chose which of their distinctive software products they wanted to buy. They didn't ask each customer what they wanted and then design software just for that customer.

Lastly, a word of warning about your own bias. Leaders often unconsciously bias their thinking about their enterprise's type by reasoning from their own approach to leadership. A chief operating officer (COO) with one of our clients, a commercial construction business, kept insisting that his enterprise was best-in-class even though his construction business was obviously a predictable and dependable enterprise, because his leadership style fit a best-in-class enterprise. Concluding that his enterprise was predictable and dependable was unconsciously (and unnecessarily) threatening to him. His boss, the CEO, was rather dictatorial, and he came to understand that this was so offensive to him that he was refusing to consider the idea that his business was inherently a predictable and dependable enterprise because, on some level, it was giving in to his boss to do so. The real issue was his disconnect with his boss.

This kind of biased thinking happens most with leaders of predictable and dependable enterprises because this enterprise and its need to stay in control is anathema to so many people. This type of enterprise has been lambasted, particularly by consultants, for over fifty years. Ironically, predictable and dependable is the most prevalent enterprise type in the developed world. It seems obvious that a utility company is a predictable and dependable enterprise, but a CEO who dislikes the idea of control may see her utility as an enrichment enterprise.

Finally, if you are a start-up and don't yet have actual customers, you can still use the process here and in the rest of this book—just ask yourself how you *will* interact with customers once you get them. If you use your enterprise type and the ideas in this book as a planning guide for building your cultural and leadership approach, you'll get a major head start in building your business.

To learn or check your enterprise type, ask yourself exactly how your enterprise behaves with customers. If the behavior is:

➤ Highly customized, personalized, tailored to each unique customer; built on a close partnership with the customer; characterized by a great deal of co-involvement with each customer each step of the way; focused on addressing the special, unique need of each customer; contingent on building a strong relationship with each customer; or the solution you offer is unique to each customer, then your customer promise is *customized*. Examples here are public relations firms, marketing consultants, executive search firms, executive coaching firms, and residential real estate companies.

➤ Providing predictable, dependable, reliable products or services; commodity/commodity-like; high-distribution intensive; providing safety, security, emergency services; providing basic necessities; linked to life and death; or providing low-cost goods; then your customer promise is *predictable and dependable*. Examples are utilities, fire and police departments, overnight delivery companies, large retailers, retail banks, and mining companies.

➤ Enrichment; helping people grow; developing and fulfilling people's potential; offering people a better, fuller, healthier life; striving to raise the human spirit; based on values, realizing ideals, higher-order purposes; or providing therapeutic products or services; then your customer promise is *enrichment*. Examples are elementary and secondary schools, therapeutic service companies, arts and entertainment companies, and enterprises built to help the less fortunate.

➤ Best-in-class; providing unparalleled products/services; providing one-of-a-kind products/services; dependent upon a high level of expertise; dependent on a high level of innovation; providing products or service that creates its own market; providing the best, most excellent products/services; contingent on unique technology or know-how; then your customer promise is *best-in-class*. Examples are high-tech companies, high-end hotel companies, medical products companies, law firms, and one-of-a-kind product companies.

Then ask yourself what your enterprise's particular combination of attention (actuality or possibility) and decision-making (impersonal or personal) is. If it is:

- Actuality and personal, then your enterprise is a customized enterprise
- Actuality and impersonal, then your enterprise is a predictable and dependable enterprise
- Possibility and personal, then your enterprise is an enrichment enterprise
- Possibility and impersonal, then your enterprise is a best-in-class enterprise

Of the approximate 41,800 people who have completed our assessments that measure enterprise types and individual leadership approach, answers to these two questions have never contradicted one another. If your answers do, read the rest of this book (or at least the chapters describing each type of enterprise!) and then determine which enterprise type is yours.

If you never learn your enterprise type, you will:

- keep dealing with the same people problems over and over
- bring in new management and leadership ideas that don't work
- struggle with strategy implementation problems
- give mixed messages to your customers
- unintentionally demoralize your employees

Determining your enterprise type will benefit you in other ways. It will center your marketing message and approach with customers, which will substantively increase your revenues. It will get you and your employees focused and on the same page and set the stage for how to lead, what kind of culture to build, whom to hire, how to manage performance, how to build your team, and much more. It will help you decide whether to merge with another enterprise and—if you decide to merge—how to do it. Details on all these topics are covered in future chapters, but it all starts with determining your enterprise type.

A Note About Our Validated Assessments

I go into our validated assessments in the Appendix, but, because I reference their use in Section II quite a bit, I think it will be helpful to you if I give you a quick picture of what they are.

There are five assessments; three of them are enterprise-level and two of them are individual-level—meaning that three of them measure what is actually happening in the enterprise and two of them measure individual characteristics. All told, the assessments took six years to originally validate (the specifics of the validation work are covered in the Appendix). Ongoing validation work continues on a regular basis. There are a total of 28,400 respondents in the enterprise-level validation efforts—covering twenty-seven enterprises. There are a total of 5,400 leaders in the individual leader–level validation efforts.

The three enterprise-level assessments are the Enterprise Customer Promise Indicator (ECPI), Enterprise Culture Indicator (ECI), and Enterprise Leadership Team Indicator (ELTI). The two individual-level assessments are the Individual Leader Indicator (ILI) and Individual Contributor Indicator (ICI).

The enterprise-level assessments are "prevalence" based. They ask a stratified sample of leaders and employees to simply indicate the extent to which (prevalence) particular behaviors are occurring in their enterprise. Put simply, respondents are asked: 1. Does your enterprise promise this (or that) to your customers? 2. Do decisions get made this way (compensation occurs this way, teaming happens this way, etc.) and, if so, to what extent? and 3. Does your senior leadership team lead this way and, if so, to what extent? The items are not right and wrong or bad and good. They simply ask people what is actually happening in their enterprise and in each unit (department) of their enterprise.

Some significant findings from our research with our assessment results are:

- 68 percent of the time, leaders view what is happening in their enterprise differently from their own employees' view of what is happening.
- 88 percent of the time, leaders and employees differ from one another about what is "core" to their enterprise and what is "support." Individual status needs clash with objective system realities.
- Compensation is treated as separate and distinct from the other fourteen cultural drivers. 55 percent of the time, compensation structure is disconnected from what the type of enterprise requires.
- Misunderstandings about the four different kinds of power create considerable frustration and confusion.
- Performance management is overly individual-centric and not enough system-centric. This leads to managing individual performance in a vacuum

2

THE PREDICTABLE AND DEPENDABLE ENTERPRISE

Providing Basic and Dependable Products and Services

➤ ➤ ➤

Astronaut Jack Swigert and mission commander Jim Lovell heard a loud bang and felt a shudder throughout the ship. Moments later, flight control received a message from Apollo 13:

"Okay, Houston, we've had a problem here."

"This is Houston. Say again please."

"Houston, we've had a problem. We've had a main B bus undervolt."

Apollo 13 was 87 hours from home and had power for 10 more hours. NASA mission control immediately took control. Technicians, engineers, and other experts were assigned to small groups, each mandated to address a particular part of the problem.

Everyone knew that time was critical. Suggestions for correcting the dropping voltage didn't work, and mission control realized that the electrical system could not be saved. They told the crew to shut down the command module to save their batteries for reentry and use the lunar module, which was equipped for two men for two days and would have to sustain three men for four. The men quickly powered down the command module and scrambled into their lunar lifeboat.

Mission Control had to get them home as fast they could while conserving power, oxygen, and water. They told the crew to change the module's trajectory and set it on course for Earth. There wasn't power to use the guidance platform's system, so the crew had to do it manually. They used special power-up procedures relayed to them by Mission Control in Houston to power the lunar module back to life so that they had enough power to get back to Earth.

Two and a half hours later they safely splashed down in the South Pacific.

NASA is a predictable and dependable enterprise. Predictable and dependable enterprises promise to provide customers with a service or product or mission—from making a moon landing to providing tap water—reliably and safely. The customer promise demands carefully measured outcomes, achieved with clear roles, policies, and procedures. So leaders in these enterprises need to provide structure, operational consistency, and direction. The culture encourages efficient, reliable systems with a hierarchical structure and constant control.

These enterprises have to be run this way. Launching men and women into space, providing germ-free tap water, and drilling for oil safely—to name just a few examples—require consistent rules and policies to operate predictably and dependably. The leaders of the Apollo 13 mission depended upon reliable data, structured rules, operational requirements, and compliance with their decisions. That is the only way to operate space missions safely; the same practices apply to all enterprises of this type, from fighting fires to flying airplanes.

Approximately 60 percent of the one hundred largest companies in America (by market capitalization) are predictable and dependable enterprises. They are necessary and have to do with life and death, safety, security, potable water, electricity, telecommunications, infrastructure, construction, mining, oil and gas, basic goods, or commodities, to name a few. The operational system in each of these enterprises has to stay in control, and many people, understandably, don't like that because they don't like being controlled. NASA's Mission Control had to take control because that was the only way the four astronauts in Apollo 13 could get back to earth. The four astronauts really liked being told how to keep the lunar module operational system in control! So, why is this kind of enterprise so disliked? This chapter will give you the answer to that.

IN THIS CHAPTER, YOU WILL LEARN:

- How exactly customers need to be approached in this kind of enterprise
- The right culture for a predictable and dependable enterprise
- How fifteen culture drivers (decision-making, hiring, performance management, compensation, and eleven more) need to be practiced
- The right leadership approach for a predictable and dependable enterprise
- How three leadership drivers need to be practiced

The Predictable and Dependable Enterprise Customer Promise and How It Must Approach Its Customers

On April 25, 2014, Flint, Michigan, switched its water supply from the Detroit system, which had served the town for fifty years, to the Flint River. The Detroit system draws its water from Lake Huron, and Flint had been using it because the Flint River was deemed unsuitable for human consumption. But the "emergency manager" appointed by Governor Rick Snyder believed that the switch would save somewhere between $6 million and $8 million.

Governor Snyder was elected, in part, because he was a former corporate CEO and venture capital entrepreneur, and people believed that he would use his business acumen to improve Michigan's finances. Governor Snyder's strategy was to appoint seven "emergency managers" to run all public entities in Michigan. These managers had complete authority to do what each believed was necessary to get the state financially sound.

Soon after the emergency manager took over Flint's water system and initiated his cost-saving idea, people began complaining that their tap water had turned brown, smelled bad, and tasted weird. People reported rashes, hair loss, bouts of hypertension, memory failure, depression, and vision loss. A research team from Virginia Tech tested the water and declared it unsafe and harmful—some homes contained lead concentrations that met the Environmental Protection Agency's definition of toxic waste. The local United Way estimates that between six thousand and twelve thousand children may have been harmed.

Since then, forty civil lawsuits have been filed on behalf of Flint residents injured by exposure to dirty water. Congressional hearings have been appointed. The FBI and the Michigan attorney general's office have initiated investigations to determine whether any public or private parties should be held criminally responsible under state or federal law. The cost of compensating the people of Flint for the injuries they have sustained will be staggering. The governor has already appropriated $232 million in state funds for short- and long-term solutions. The costs that will accrue to the children and families harmed will last for the rest of their lives.

So much for saving $6 million to $8 million!

There are many aspects to what happened in Flint. I want to highlight one. Every water utility, everywhere, is fundamentally a predictable and dependable enterprise. People need clean, safe, potable water, consistently provided 24/7. The water system has to be predictable—people depend on this system to stay alive. That is the promise that every municipal water enterprise makes to every customer.

We have worked with fourteen utilities in our assessment database— three water utilities, four electric utilities, three wastewater utilities and four telephone utilities. We asked each utility's leaders and employees to complete a multiple-choice assessment describing their customer promise. Their choices were descriptors such as "one-of-kind product or service," "highly customized product or service," "raise the human spirit," and "high level of safety and security." They all chose "high level of safety and security."

But those in charge of Flint's water did not have this clear understanding. They did not seem to know that their utility's only purpose was to provide safe, clean, healthy, and potable water to Flint's citizens. Thus, they ill-advisedly put saving $6 million to $8 million ahead of providing clean, safe, potable water to the Flint community. Had they understood the essential nature of a utility, the idea of risking the quality and safety of Flint's water wouldn't even have come up for discussion.

In his March, 2016 testimony before Congress, Governor Snyder testified that "from now on we are going to put clean, safe water first and foremost. That's why I am so committed to delivering permanent, long-term solutions and the clean, safe drinking water that every Michigan citizen deserves." Why would he ever even have considered doing anything else?

Flint's water utility—or any predictable and dependable enterprise— delivers on its customer promise with efficient systems and clear policies and procedures. This is completely different from how things are done in an enrichment enterprise. At Habitat for Humanity, for example, the employees can often decide what job they believe they can do best, because they believe in the enterprise's values and are committed to acting in accordance with them. Employees in a water utility can't possibly make those kinds of decisions for themselves. Each employee has to implement the very specific function that will deliver on the utility's customer promise. Operational system effectiveness counts most in delivering on a customer promise in a predictable and dependable enterprise. Goodwill counts most in delivering on customer promise in an enrichment enterprise. Thus, the two enterprise types need different leadership and different cultures.

The predictable and dependable enterprise centers its attention on what is actually occurring in present time. It must deliver on its customer promise now, immediately. Fires need to be put out now so firefighters have to rely on protocols, rules, systematic procedures, pre-determined requirements. Police need to respond as quickly as possible and decide by the facts before them. Utilities must provide water or energy or telecommunications 24/7.

Big-box retailers must have continuous control over inventories, distribution channels, and shipping. Customers walk into a Walmart store expecting that the goods they are interested in buying are there on the shelves *now*.

One way to understand each enterprise is to look at it in comparison and contrast to the other three enterprises. Figure 2-1 shows what each enterprise is offering.

Figure 2-1. Offering of Each of the Four Living Enterprises

The predictable and dependable enterprise promises to meet a basic need, usually one common to everyone. Examples of "basic needs" are safe and healthy water, rescue from a fire, safety from harm, basic necessities, energy, transport, and much more. A wide range of enterprises fall into the predictable and dependable category. Big-box retailers like Walmart, utilities, police and fire departments, retail banks, airlines, big delivery companies like Federal Express, miners, oil and gas companies, distribution companies like pipeline companies, credit card companies, telephone companies, automobile companies, fast-food restaurants, grocery companies, construction companies, and cable companies are all examples. So are AT&T's Universal Card, William Wrigley Jr. Company, Kellogg Company, Procter & Gamble, Dell Computer, United Airlines, and Amazon.

Given the nature of commerce, this enterprise is, by far, the most prevalent in developed economies. Predictable and dependable enterprises cover the waterfront of basic needs. They are typically utilitarian in nature. They tend to be highly capital-intensive, low-margin, and low-to-moderate cost. Most are huge in size and continually strive for more and more market share dominance. To a considerable extent, this is rather inevitable given their low margins and economies of scale. Walmart, for example, as of early 2016, has 11,527 stores and clubs in twenty-seven countries. In 2014, it was the world's largest company by revenue and the world's biggest private employer with 2.2 million employees.

Many of these enterprises assume that their customers are satisfied when they don't hear from them. No news is good news. At these enterprises, the majority of customer calls are complaints. So, ironically, when they don't hear from customers they assume customers are happy. These enterprises also receive calls when customers do not understand something about the company's procedures or their own responsibilities. Predictable and dependable enterprises try to head these kinds of calls off at the pass by providing online information or including information letters with invoices. Utilities, for example, rarely meet customers face-to-face more than once (if that) or talk to them. This is normally fine with customers who, typically, are in a hurry or just need one bit of information from the company.

Predictable and dependable enterprises have been criticized as old-fashioned and harmful for fifty years or more. They have been called toxic, destructive, anti-innovative, breeders of sycophants, crippling, and demeaning. It is true that employees in these enterprises are often overly controlled, ordered around by bosses, just told what to do and not listened to. That's because these enterprises can easily get out of balance and, when they do, they disempower their people. (See Chapter 10 for a discussion of balance.)

Despite people's disgust for these enterprises, they persist, because they meet basic and necessary needs. In order to do this, they build and preserve an operational system. At the end of the day, they will fail if they don't. Both leaders and employees must implement the most effective operational system that they can and keep the system in control—that's the most important part of their jobs. People are important, but their role is to ensure that the enterprise's operational system functions effectively. That is what delivers on the enterprise's customer promise and determines the right kind of culture and leadership for the enterprise.

Of the four kinds of enterprises, the predictable and dependable enterprise is definitely the most prone to disempowering its people. Leaders must prevent that from happening and remain aware of how likely it is to happen.

Take a nuclear power plant. It simply has to have an operation that is in control at all times. It has to be regulated and very ordered. It has to operate in a prescribed manner 24 hours a day, 7 days a week, 365 days a year. It is required to operate this way in order to deliver on its promise to its customers. Decisions are made based on evidence, data, facts, gauges, meters, and objective measurements. Of the four enterprises, this kind of enterprise is by far the most impersonal in nature. So, it is the most prone to objectifying its people and demanding specific behaviors. In order for its people to be treated with the importance that they deserve, leaders must stay vigilant about preventing their objectification.

It isn't only employees who get objectified—customers do too. Utilities frequently call customers "ratepayers." Other predictable and dependable enterprises call their customers "consumers," "citizens," "targets," "users," "buyers," "shoppers," and "passengers." Leaders of predictable and dependable enterprises need to be vigilant about preventing their customers from being taken for granted and objectified.

Four processes that relate to how customers are approached—pricing, sales, planning, and budgeting—are practiced differently in each of the four enterprises. Pricing in predictable and dependable enterprises relies on economies of scale. Enterprises with this customer promise typically build and operate facilities for high-volume, repetitive operational tasks. High fixed costs make large volumes essential to achieving low unit cost, so making the right pricing decisions is important. These decisions are often distribution intensive, as they are in grocery companies. Commodity- and convenience-oriented enterprises—typically, predictable and dependable enterprises—have customers who consistently expect prices to be low.

Sales, in the typical sense of that word, barely exist in predictable and dependable enterprises and is often something of a misnomer. When was the last time you had a "salesperson" from your electric utility pay you a visit? Or from McDonald's, Federal Express, or your local post office? Many years ago, I started working with a gas pipeline company, and, after a few visits, I asked the VP of Human Resources where the marketing and sales departments were. He said, "Follow me," and we went down the elevator of the building to the basement. He walked me over to two very small, empty rooms with card tables and chairs in each and a light bulb hanging from each ceiling and said, "This one is our marketing department and this one is our sales department." As I came to learn, the real salespeople for the company were the attorneys who did all of the negotiating with gas producers and gas utilities. In many of these enterprises, selling boils down to "here it is and this is what it costs."

Predictable and dependable enterprises are usually very capital intensive—Exxon's capital spending budget in 2014 was $35.8 billion. Planning (long range, intermediate range, and short term) capability is crucial. Poor planning can put you in the poor house. Budgeting also plays a central role because so many predictable and dependable enterprises run on thin margins.

Pricing, planning, budgeting, and sales in predictable and dependable enterprises are impersonal. Leaders and managers need information about their customers, but they rarely meet with them. Utilities typically price, plan, budget, and announce (their equivalent of "selling") without ever coming face-to-face with any customers.

This has major implications about how this kind of enterprise approaches its customers. At a minimum, it has to go out of its way to proactively connect with them and incorporate their thinking into the practice of these four processes. Any enterprise that skips this step, as many do, runs the risk of alienating its customers.

The Right Culture for a Predictable and Dependable Enterprise and How Fifteen Cultural Drivers Must Be Practiced

IBM's mainframe computers and PCs once led the industry. The mainframes were huge, expensive energy hogs. In the late 1970s, one typical IBM mainframe computer took up the whole floor of an office building—or house! I once met an information technology business executive who bought an old IBM mainframe computer and knocked all the walls down on the second floor of his house so the mainframe would fit.

Because Apple's personal computer (PC) was so successful, IBM created an "IBM PC" unit and—to keep it separate from its mainframe business in Armonk, New York—located it in Boca Raton, Florida. Senior leadership wanted to give the new unit room to grow on its own, without being smothered by the mainframe mother ship in Armonk. They believed that as an independent business, the new unit could innovate more freely and outdistance the competition (which was avidly heating up) more quickly. They also installed a separate sales unit in Boca Raton and made certain that sales unit was completely dedicated to marketing and selling the IBM PC.

That was a wise decision. The IBM PC was an immense success. The day IBM announced its PC, 40,000 people ordered one. By the end of 1982, IBM was selling a PC a minute. It didn't take long for IBM to capture more market share than all of its competitors.

Then, the home office decided to shut down the PC unit in Boca Raton and bring the PC business to headquarters in Armonk.

The culture in Armonk was a control culture, the kind of culture that fits a predictable and dependable customer promise. It had a hierarchical structure. Decisions were made by those at the highest level, compensation was tied to hierarchical level, and work was entirely functional in nature (meaning that the hierarchy consisted of particular functions like manufacturing, finance, sales, etc.).

Boca Raton, however, was a competence culture, the kind that fits a best-in-class customer promise. It had a matrix structure and was organized by expertise (specialists) and computer hardware components (hard drive group, keyboard group, memory group, etc.). Each group had the exact kind of experts required for each hardware component. This is the matrix structure often used by best-in-class enterprises. It is very different from the hierarchical structure used in Armonk—and at most predictable and dependable enterprises. Compensation in Boca Raton was incentivized. The more your component group achieved, the more money you made.

The Boca Raton salespeople had to be much more versatile than their counterparts in Armonk because they were principally selling to established retail companies (like RadioShack). Armonk sold directly to end users (other businesses). Because Armonk's buyer was another company, the sales process was very structured and prescripted. Selling to retail companies, as the PC group did, was a completely different process. But the sales groups were merged, too, and had to follow the mainframe, end user sales process, which didn't fit with what it took to sell to retailers.

When the PC unit joined the mainframe group in Armonk, it had to adapt. In Armonk, decisions were made at the top of the hierarchy—by people with high-level titles (vice president, senior vice president, president, etc.). In the PC unit, the experts were the main deciders. As you might guess, the home office's way of deciding undermined the future growth of the PC business because it took much, much longer for decisions to get made and when they finally were made, many were wrong.

The experts became demoralized. They saw that in Armonk, titles counted, not expertise. The unit's best experts left and went to competitors who were also competence cultures. In effect, the home office was unknowingly helping the competition beat IBM in the marketplace.

Conflict was mismanaged, too. When people in the PC unit differed with the home office on an issue, the conflict was "resolved" by people above them in the hierarchy, rather than by the people who disagreed and argued until they reached the right solution. Those "resolving" the conflict in Armonk were not even experts in the personal computer business. Most of these resolutions didn't resolve anything and, indeed, created a whole new set of conflicts that hadn't existed (for either party) before. Frustration spread, which led to more conflicts between experts and their bosses. Additional conflicts were created because unresolved conflicts persisted and caused poorer performance. These conflicts compounded. People in the PC unit were promoted and, thereby, given more power because they fit the mold of the home office, not because they were effective managers of a diverse set of experts (which calls for a whole unique set of behaviors that aren't called for in a control culture). This created more frustration.

The architecture of the unit morphed into the architecture of the home office. The matrix organizational structure was replaced by a hierarchy. This had a major negative effect on workflow, quality of decision-making, and speed of performance. The latter was particularly problematic because the personal computer business was then (and is now!) fast and furious—new competitors come into the marketplace fast, necessitating faster development of better PC features and quick-to-market presence in the marketplace.

The nature of the work changed. Experts were required to meet the demands of a function (e.g., research and development) rather than a product. Home office pulled research and development toward long plans that, among other things, required much more time and many multileveled reviews. Before the move, the PC unit did much more experimenting. It used trial and error. Those in the PC unit tested in the real world—and designed PC products much more quickly in Boca Rotan than they could in Armonk. Teaming was different, too. In Boca Raton, teams were quite ad hoc and responded quickly to marketplace demands. They were project-oriented; when the project was completed, they disbanded. Each team was composed of carefully selected experts who moved from one team to another. Conflict was part of a team's process, as teams struggled to get things right—teaming was usually "win-lose."

By contrast, teaming in the home office was cross-functional—meaning that people from different functions were placed on a team that worked on cross-functional issues (e.g., between R&D and manufacturing). These teams remained in place for very long times. Conflict was taboo. The rule was: Head it off at the pass and prevent it from ever occurring. Each team was focused on ensuring that the operational process worked the way it was supposed to work. Priorities for hiring got confused. In the PC unit, a matrix-structured team of experts decided whom to hire. In the home office, the manager of a function made the final decision about whom to hire.

Contradictions in development cropped up—both in content and method. Training in the home office was formal, structured, and focused on functional needs. In the unit, training occurred simultaneously with implementation and focused on the expertise needed in real time. The same kinds of differences occurred regarding innovation and the management of change. Home office's control culture worked to engineer away the need for change on the front end. Change was to be either avoided or baked into plans that ensured that change was controlled from beginning to end. In the unit, change, innovation, and people development were an ongoing part of every day's work. The home office worked to avoid or control change; the unit expected it to be a key part of its ability to outdistance the competition.

A year after the PC group joined the mainframe computer group, IBM's PC business went into a slow decline, and that decline persisted until the company sold its entire PC business to Lenovo (a Chinese company) in 2004. At the time of the sale, IBM had 5 percent of the PC market.

While there were several factors that contributed to the IBM PC's decline, a major factor was the clash of culture between the home office and the Boca Raton unit.

IBM's home office was not some "evil kingdom" that was out to destroy IBM's burgeoning PC business. The home office had a time-worn (and successful) control culture that practiced fifteen cultural elements in the manner required for the enterprise to deliver on its promise to its mainframe computer customers. The idea that the PC unit in Boca Raton had a different customer promise and, therefore, IBM needed to simply allow the PC unit to continue doing what it had been doing so well never even occurred to senior leadership. When IBM's senior leaders decided to bring the PC unit into the home office, their stated goal was to "build continuity." That is exactly what a predictable and dependable enterprise would do and should do. The best-in-class enterprise, however, does not need hierarchical and functional structure–it needs freedom to imagine new and different products and services, freedom to experiment and to fail and to move fast. Failure is prevented and headed off at the pass in a predictable and dependable enterprise; it is required in a best-in-class enterprise because failure tells you what is not working.

The predictable and dependable enterprise requires a control culture in order to deliver on its particular customer promise. Enterprises with this promise emphasize producing consistent results by building and operating a highly efficient system. The fundamental issue in a control culture is to preserve, grow, and ensure the success of the enterprise's operational system per se. Operations comes first and requires predictability, dependability, and standardization. Accordingly, the design and framework for information and knowledge in this enterprise is built essentially around the operational goals of the enterprise, and the extent to which those goals are met. Performance is managed to accomplish operational goals; production and verifiable performance hold center stage. Policies and procedures abound. This culture is centered on operational goal attainment. To meet that goal, it needs to stay in control.

The predictable and dependable enterprise is typically structured in a hierarchical manner where teamwork equals the effective use of cross-functional capabilities. It is no-nonsense, serious, realistic, and matter-of-fact. Not much speculation goes on. Discipline and definitiveness are important. Considerable emphasis is placed on objective information and data that can be relied upon.

Given its content and process nature, this culture is highly task oriented, particularly where daily tasks are concerned. Getting the job done on a consistent, regular, and current basis is very important. Strong emphasis is placed on rules and adherence to them.

Functionalists (people who are capable of performing a specific function) hold center stage in this culture. Compensation is typically tied to operational goal attainment, functional performance, power, and position. It is a world built on adherence to role requirements in the interest of operational success.

Decision-making is very factual, data based, detached, and methodical. Most thinking is cause-to-effect, objective, and conservative. This enterprise takes risks that are carefully considered, thoroughly researched, and rigorously tested for viability and risk vs. reward. Its approach to managing change is to anticipate it and neutralize it or to build it into a plan so it is manageable.

The Right Leadership for a Predictable and Dependable Enterprise and How Three Leadership Drivers Must Be Practiced

When senior leadership decided to fold its PC unit into the home office, IBM was prospering and its directive leadership had led the company to success; in fact, it was the most successful mainframe computer company in the world. It employed 342,000 people. It was a predictable and dependable enterprise with a vertically integrated strategy, building most components of its systems itself, including processors, operating systems, peripherals, databases, and the like. This strategy alone pulled it into the shape of a control culture. Its leadership approach was directive, which is the approach a predictable and dependable customer promise requires, and by 1980, had been working well for seventy years.

The leadership set the company's direction by thinking long term, establishing realistically achievable goals, and building highly detailed plans to attain them. Goal setting started with what the enterprise had accomplished already and projected growth from there. Company-wide goals and plans were developed first and then cascaded down throughout the rest of the company—function by function. Financial goals, competitor analyses, analyses of threats and opportunities were developed. Each plan built by different functions was reviewed and approved by senior management. Contingency plans were developed at all levels. It was a given that any new product would take at least four years to develop. The PC unit's planning was much more iterative and short-term focused. The evolving capability of the product itself and features that gave it a distinct competitive advantage drove goal setting and plans to achieve those goals. The PC marketplace demanded quick development.

IBM leadership at headquarters fostered commitment within the enterprise by emphasizing the preservation of tradition, bringing order and stability into the organization, and ensuring focus on attaining operational goals. Headquarters systematically tracked operational goal attainment and celebrated success all along the way and let people know that their contributions were appreciated.

The PC unit's leadership fostered commitment by celebrating each component of product development, no matter how small, and celebrating each sale, big or small.

Lastly, IBM leadership at headquarters built organizational capability by building an authoritative infrastructure, building operational systems, and developing policies and procedures. They also built support systems that fostered the success of the operational core of the business. The PC unit leaders built organizational capability by managing the relationship between the home office and the unit, building an expertise-based infrastructure, and ensuring that people could continually innovate. They set high standards and challenged people to keep doing better and better.

Armonk's ways were right for a predictable and dependable enterprise, which requires directive leadership. Directive leadership is essentially a matter of fully understanding one's marketplace and building an operational system that ensures the attainment of important operational goals. The directive leader attaches great importance to planning and goal setting. This leader treats planning as the way to stay in control. Very often, the emphasis is on market share dominance.

Goals and objectives are realistic and, more often than not, primarily utilitarian. Goals are often oriented toward precise measures of input to output. This leader works hard to ensure that goals and objectives are clearly understood while emphasizing the accomplishment of concrete, immediate, and tangible results.

Decision-making is data based and objective. Predictable and reliable operational functioning is the key to the success of this enterprise and, as a result, this leader places considerable emphasis on adherence to role requirements. Clear policies and procedures are established because they are crucial to effective performance. Order and stability are emphasized. Input from subordinates typically comes in the form of reports and detailed analyses. Decision-making is thorough, methodical, and systematic; it usually takes a long time to gather and analyze the facts before deciding. People follow a directive leader because they have confidence in his or her understanding of the actions needed for the organization to succeed. He or she has demonstrated knowledge of effective organizational functioning in the past.

There are several important messages in this chapter that, historically, haven't gotten the attention that they deserve. First, good leaders in predictable and dependable enterprises are not insensitive bullies who enjoy pushing people around. They must lead in a directive manner—their customer promise requires it. They are responsible for ensuring that the operational system of their enterprise stays *in control*, runs consistently and efficiently, and prevents as many errors as possible. In many instances, lives depend on this happening.

The important message in this chapter that frequently gets missed is that in a predictable and dependable enterprise, it is the system that needs to be in control, not the people. Employees need to be led in a way that empowers them to be "co-controllers" (with leaders) of the system. A leader who behaves as a dictator only increases the risk factor(s) that go with the particular kind of system that he is operating. The system focus underpins the success of a fire department. Firemen are rigorously trained and prepared. Once they are on the scene of a fire, they use a proven system for putting it out. They don't need someone to tell each of them what to do, every second. They have been ingrained in the system and, therefore, know what to do. Leaders and employees in a predictable and dependable enterprise need to co–problem solve, co-operate (pun intended), co-monitor, and co-control the system. Requiring firefighters on the scene of a fire to follow constant demands from a boss every step of the way only increases the likelihood that they will not put out the fire. Some leaders in predictable and dependable enterprises don't understand this distinction and order people around. Not surprisingly, when this occurs, employees (and other leaders) don't like it, and their dictatorial behavior gets in the way of delivering on the enterprise's customer promise.

As discussed earlier, quite a number of people over the years have completely disparaged this enterprise. From the perspective of this book, they are throwing the baby out with the bathwater.

The second message is that because the operational system is so central in this enterprise, leaders have to be vigilant about proactively empowering their people. It is impossible to imagine that robots could replace many of the people in the other three kinds of enterprises, but it is not hard to imagine that in this enterprise—precisely because it is so regimented and routinized and so operational system-based. Take a look at one of Amazon's fulfillment centers, if you would like an example. As of the third quarter of 2015, Amazon has 30,000 robots deployed in its U.S. warehouses and fulfillment centers. The company also has big plans to use drones (not people) to deliver packages to customers.

The mindset that devised and implemented 30,000 robots in its fulfillment centers and warehouses will, inevitably, be tempted to mechanize and control its people. That is already happening. Amazon workers are all told stories of people who have been fired for theft; flat-screen TVs display examples. Each employee fired is shown as a black silhouette stamped with the word terminated, and details of when they stole, what they stole, how much it was worth, and how they got caught are displayed. Putting the Orwellian cast of this to the side, this response on Amazon's part is entirely predictable. It is probably safe to say that Amazon executives spend a lot more time mechanizing the business than stewarding the development of their people (an enrichment enterprise instinct) and, therefore, default to a "control" solution to theft and most other problems. Trying to stop thievery by scaring and threatening your whole workforce (most of whom are, presumably, not thieves) will not work and will cause more problems. Amazon would be well advised to connect with the people in its warehouses and fulfillment centers and get *their* thinking about how to reduce theft.

The main message here is that, because it is a predictable and dependable enterprise, Amazon should devote managerial attention to encouraging and developing people, rather than controlling their every move. Their "in control" operational system mindset is already dominating the business—there is no need to extend it to all areas of their employees' behavior. Strengths that are overused or misapplied turn into weaknesses.

The predictable and dependable enterprise has many strengths. It is usually very effective at planning, spotting problems and heading them off at the pass, and project management. If you are in a high-risk business like catching criminals, putting out fires, or launching rockets, this is the kind of enterprise you want to build. It doesn't get surprised much. It is inherently realistic and practical. Expectations, roles, and jobs are clear. The danger in this kind of enterprise is that it can slip into over-control and/or unnecessary control. Leaders in this enterprise need to proactively ensure that employees are empowered to co-control the system and to prevent leaders and managers from believing that their job is to control their employees. Leaders who over-control their employees will get unpleasantly surprised about an operational system problem because those over-controlled employees were afraid to come and tell them when they spotted it.

3

THE ENRICHMENT ENTERPRISE
Elevating Customers' Lives

➤ ➤ ➤

When I describe the enrichment enterprise to businesspeople, people don't react the way they do to descriptions of the predictable and dependable, best-in-class, or customized enterprise. I get blank stares or comments like "this kind of enterprise doesn't apply to business," or "this is really just about a start-up company," or "spending time on do-gooder enterprises isn't my cup of tea," or "this just applies to the nonprofit world." Sometimes, people are immediately put off by the mention of this enterprise because they believe it is an opening to a call for "social justice" or a rail against capitalism. What I get the most is avoidance—a kind of "I don't want to go there."

For quite a few businesspeople, the enrichment enterprise is incongruent with the conduct of business. Yet, there are quite a number of endeavors that are enrichment and also for-profit, such as KinderCare, Tom's Shoes, The Body Shop, Patagonia, rehabilitation centers, assisted living companies, and many others.

More dangerous to enrichment enterprises is that most business schools and many consultants believe that these enterprises should be primarily focused on profit goals. Once, Habitat for Humanity (H4H) brought in a highly respected business consulting firm because people were unclear about responsibilities and duplicating work. The consulting firm proposed that H4H develop a new business model with a metricized strategic and operational plan and a financial plan. H4H agreed and, with the consulting firm's help, began implementing the plans.

The operational plan called for more central control, a hierarchical structure, job descriptions, and a performance management system. The financial plan set revenue goals, cost control goals, and retained earnings goals. All this met with considerable resistance. People said it was busywork keeping them from doing their jobs and that it was much too controlling. After much discussion, H4H leaders came to agree.

The plans were trying to turn H4H into a top-down, centrally controlled, functionally structured enterprise. But that took people off course and actually got in the way, rather than taking the enterprise ahead. So the plans were all scrapped.

Without knowing it, the consulting firm had tried to turn H4H into a predictable and dependable enterprise. The predictable and dependable enterprise is the exact opposite of an enrichment enterprise. An enrichment enterprise exists to realize people's *values or beliefs*, not to build and maintain operational systems.

Habitat for Humanity is a grassroots enterprise. It grew organically, over many years, one community at a time. Trying to change it into a top-down, central control, hierarchical enterprise with job descriptions and functions only served to pull the enterprise off center and create more confusion. Putting financial goals front and center really confused things. Staying financially solvent was obviously important, but in an enrichment enterprise, finance and accounting must operate in service to the core. The core of Habitat for Humanity had to focus on realizing its values and beliefs, while finance and accounting had to help the core stay financially solvent. Putting financial and accounting goals first was a major contradiction and set up crosscurrents in the enterprise that caused more problems.

IN THIS CHAPTER, READERS WILL LEARN:

- How exactly customers need to be approached in this kind of enterprise
- The right culture for an enrichment enterprise
- How fifteen culture drivers (decision-making, hiring, performance management, compensation, and eleven more) need to be practiced in a enrichment enterprise

- The right leadership approach for a enrichment enterprise
- How three leadership drivers need to be practiced

The Enrichment Enterprise Customer Promise and How It Must Approach Its Customers

Ellen Swanson was proud of her work at Kids First (pseudonym), a sizable chain of day care centers, and both her students and their parents appreciated her. During her seven years there, Kids First grew by leaps and bounds. With that growth came considerable central control from corporate headquarters.

Ellen went from being autonomous to being told to "meet her teacher-student ratio quota," regularly complete reports, help the center "meet its revenue and profit goals," and work to find ways to cut costs. Her compensation became tied entirely to her teacher-student ratio quota and the center's revenues and profits. Students were routinely moved around from one class to another in order to meet the ratio.

Center managers roamed all the classrooms every day to ask: "How many students do you have today, what's your number, how many more kids do you expect to come in today?" If any teachers were "over labor," they were told to "cut hours." Teacher turnover increased and parents complained. Then, at an all-teacher meeting, the teachers were told that they would have to start paying for the crayons, paper, and other supplies the children used in their classrooms. Ellen resigned the next day. Thirty percent of the other teachers resigned in the same year, and 23 percent of the parents removed their children.

Senior leadership at Kids First, Inc., has the perfect leadership formula for going out of business. While they control one set of costs, they are escalating others—costs to acquire more customers and costs to recruit, hire, and train more teachers, among others. If current trends continue and they cannot quickly replace the 23 percent of parents they have lost in the last twelve months, they have only four years left in business.

Every day care center is an enrichment enterprise—it promises to help customers (children and their parents who serve as proxies for their children) have fuller, better lives, to help them develop and fulfill their potential. It is not a predictable and dependable enterprise, which promises consistency and reliability and operates in a controlled and directed way in order to deliver on that promise. Kids First's leaders are using a leadership and cultural model that fits a nuclear power plant, but not a day care center.

An enrichment enterprise is values centered. A parent who places her child in a day care center is expecting its leaders and teachers to care for and help develop her child. She values the growth of her child. The more that care and development occurs, the more successful the company! Parents are not expecting (much less, paying) to have their children moved around from room to room to meet numerical quotas. Parents and their children do not want to be called and treated as "ratepayers."

A predictable and dependable enterprise primarily utilizes data, facts, numbers, policies, rules, etc. to make decisions. Its decision-making process is impersonal. An enrichment enterprise uses people's judgment and values to make decisions. The decision-making process is personal. Care and development cannot be reduced to numerical data; data have little or nothing to do with what matters in a day care center. What *does* matter in decision-making is the *judgment* of parents and teachers. That's messier, but that's just the way things are in enrichment enterprises. Placing finance and accounting at the helm of a day care center business can only take the enterprise off course and guarantee its eventual failure.

In an enrichment enterprise, finance and accounting are support functions that need to operate in service to the delivery of the business's enrichment customer promise. True, the enterprise must operate in a reasonably profitable manner. What this means in a day care center is that the finance and accounting functions need to come up with information that helps keep the enterprise afloat and enhances its ability to deliver on its promise to parents. And, these two functions need to do this *for* the teachers, not tell the teachers to do it for them!

You cannot mechanize the development of a child. Centering everyone's behavior on trying to monetize the development of a child will cause a day care center to lose money. If a day care company's leaders primarily treat their teachers as cost items on a P&L statement, they are crippling the source of their enterprise's success.

So, what should Kids First's senior executives be doing? They should behave as catalysts and enablers, not controllers. They should center their behavior on empowering leaders and teachers in the centers to deliver on their promise of enrichment. Decisions about how to develop the children under their care should be made by each center's teachers.

Enterprises that are dedicated to helping the less fortunate are enrichment enterprises. Habitat for Humanity's vision is "a world where everyone has a decent place to live." Habitat for Humanity has more than 1,400 local affiliates in the United States and more than 70 national organizations around the world. It has helped 6.8 million people improve their living conditions since it was founded in 1976. The American Red Cross, another enrichment enterprise, "prevents and alleviates human suffering in the face of emergencies by mobilizing the power of volunteers and the generosity of donors."

Enrichment enterprises are premised on the notion that customers are paying for a fuller, better life. These enterprises help people fulfill their potential, to be all they can be. For example, the Ranch at Live Oak in Malibu, California, describes itself as a "fitness/wellness immersion" enterprise. Its mission is to "create a space for personal inspiration and life transformation." The staff there are "dedicated to creating a safe, secure and sacred place to allow for personal awareness and life transformation; physically, mentally and spiritually."

After one week at the Ranch, one of the Ranch's patrons wrote to the staff: "This was an amazing week. All of you did a great job. My experience here exceeded all of my expectations. I think what I appreciate the most are the new perspectives it provided me towards what I am capable of and how I prioritize things in my life. My heartfelt thanks to you and the program's designers. This has been a life-changing experience." The Ranch at Live Oaks delivered on its customer promise!

Additional examples of enrichment enterprises are elementary schools, secondary schools, many universities and colleges, health and wellness centers, rehabilitation and treatment centers, spas, certain kinds of retailers, foundations, therapeutic products and/or services, and the arts.

Jos de Blok is the founder and director of Buurtzorg Nederland, a nonprofit enterprise. Buurtzorg provides home healthcare to the elderly and the sick and is the largest neighborhood nursing organization in the Netherlands. It started as a team of 4 nurses in 2006 and, as of this writing, has grown to 8,000. It serves 50,000 patients and has revenue of more than €180 million. It has received numerous awards, including national Employer of the Year.

Jos started Buurtzorg because he was dissatisfied with traditional home healthcare enterprises. He was tired of bureaucracies, nurses working in isolation from other care providers, and treatment decisions being made by people with administrative titles. Partly because caregivers were paid by the hour and each caregiver performed only one type of task, each patient had far too many different caregivers.

So, he developed a new model: skilled nurses working together in a team of no more than twelve, in a neighborhood of 10,000 people, caring for all kinds of patients. These teams were fully responsible for the patients and had complete autonomy to deliver the best possible care. The enterprise had very low overhead costs so the money could be spent on the patients and their nurses. Those providing the care were supported by an IT system and a single 'back office' of thirty people. Jos is the only person in the enterprise with a managerial title.

Nurses are fully empowered and have the central role in the enterprise because they know best about how to treat their patients. Buurtzorg's customer promise is "to change and improve the delivery and quality of home health care through the leadership and collaboration of the community nurse, allowing the individual to receive the kind of care they most need, where they most want it, and thus avoid more costly institutional care for as long as possible."

Buurtzorg is a clear example of an enrichment enterprise's customer promise. Enterprises with this kind of customer promise are premised on the notion that their customers are paying for personal enrichment. Enrichment enterprises believe in enhancing the growth, health, or well-being of the customer.

Religious organizations are enrichment organizations—they bring purpose into people's lives. They are dedicated to raising the human spirit, inculcating ethics and values, and uplifting humankind. They strive to further the realization of ideals, values, and higher-order purposes.

Some retail enterprises are enrichment. Anita Roddick started The Body Shop with the idea that "business could be a force for good." The company's "manifesto" is "to enrich, not exploit—enriching people as well as our planet." Patagonia's mission is to "build the best product, cause no unnecessary harm, use business to inspire and implement solutions to the environmental crisis."

Enrichment customers expect improvement in their quality of life, health, or physical well-being. Treatment centers (e.g., physical therapy), rehabilitation centers, and home healthcare are enrichment. So are enterprises that provide therapeutic products and/or services for culture and the arts. They improve people's lives, provide people with different ways of thinking and teach and uplift people. Pre-school, elementary, and secondary schools and most universities are enrichment enterprises. Montessori schools began educating children in the early 20th century and now have schools all around the world. Their promise is "to guide children on the path of true discovery, to enhance independence, inspiration, and intelligence."

The central focus for enrichment enterprises is *value-centered goal attainment*. Their promise to their customers is rooted in values, faith, and deeply held beliefs. To a large extent, enrichment enterprises are centered on possibilities.

The guiding blueprint for these enterprises is to clarify the behaviors and results they need to see in order to assess how well they are realizing their values. Doing this assessment is straightforward for organizations like Habitat for Humanity—it's not hard to see whether or not they have built houses for homeless families. It's more complicated for enterprises that, for example, teach children, but the assessment can still be done. The first step is to be clear about the enterprise's values and what those realized values *actually look like in behavior.*

Planning is relatively straightforward for treatment centers, treatment-related enterprises, and retailers. Goals are set, plans are built, progress is monitored, etc. In most other kinds of enrichment enterprises, planning tends to be resisted. Leaders and employees in these enterprises need to build plans, because plans establish expectations and serve as a guide for going forward. Goals need to be formulated and their attainment needs to be tracked because this sets parameters for people and provides the framework for celebrating when goals are attained. Doing this also keeps workloads manageable in an environment where people tend to take on too much and get overloaded.

Much like the customized enterprise (which provides a tailored product or service for each unique customer), an enrichment enterprise is very often a difficult business to scale. If it is nonprofit and relies on contributions, growth depends upon the good will and generosity of other people. Finding donors is difficult and takes a great deal of time. Growth comes slowly and, in most cases, will inevitably level off for even the most successful enrichment enterprise—there is a limited supply of co-believers.

How prices are set varies widely in enrichment enterprises. In quite a few, such as Habitat for Humanity, customers do not pay anything. When it comes to tuition pricing, parents and students, at present, are in a "take-it-or-leave-it" position. For retailers, treatment or treatment-related centers, pricing boils down to what the market will bear. Treatment or treatment-related centers and retail enterprises have the most room to scale.

Many public elementary and secondary schools and many universities rely on contributions, taxes, tuition, or some mix of all three. Taxes as a source of funding are always iffy for political, societal, and monetary supply reasons.

Marketing and sales for nonprofit, contribution-dependent enterprises are essentially equivalent to fund-raising. Marketing and sales for tax-dependent schools and universities entail deploying public relations, lobbying, and convincing legislators. Most for-profit schools, treatment centers, treatment-related enterprises, and retailers mirror what happens with other kinds of enterprises.

An enrichment enterprise's customers don't need to be convinced of benefits. It's obvious that what the company offers will benefit them: homes for the homeless, education for children and young people, renewed health, goods that protect the environment, operas for opera lovers, care for the wounded, spiritual growth for religious believers. Sales and marketing essentially equate to getting the word out.

However, when these rely on contributors and donors or taxes, budgeting is important. Enrichment enterprises often get too caught up in their mission and don't pay enough attention to budgeting. Roughly around 2010, several YMCA centers in the city where I live had to shut down. When asked what went wrong, one of the center directors said: "We had way too much mission and not enough margin."

If you want to know how an enterprise is most likely to get into trouble, look at its diametric opposite. Enrichment enterprises struggle with control, structure, and quantitative matters like cost control and efficiency—all central elements in a predictable and dependable enterprise. But at an enrichment enterprise, people feel guilty when they can't provide what they believe in so strongly and good intentions prevail over practicalities like the budget.

Plus, people who work in these kinds of enterprises often just flat out dislike having to deal with budget issues. To counteract that, these enterprises should try to concentrate as much as possible on the cost side of the ledger and keep "administrative" costs to a bare minimum. Those responsible for budgeting should do as much of the cost-watching and cost-reducing as they can *for* the people who are directly delivering on the enterprise's customer promise (i.e., not burden them with forms, report requirements, and other administrative tasks). At treatment centers, treatment-related enterprises, and retailers, this isn't so important: Those enterprises can be administered the way most other kinds of enterprises are.

When a for-profit enrichment enterprise is publicly traded, the concomitant forces will very often cause major disconnections. Much like the customized enterprise, the nature of what it takes to deliver on the enrichment customer promise clashes with investor expectations—particularly consistent growth, year-over-year improvement, and consistent profit growth. It then becomes very difficult for the enrichment enterprise to resist the pressure to default to central control. As this continues, executives and shareholders often emerge as the *real* customers. Kids First, discussed at the beginning of this chapter, illustrates what usually happens next—delivering on the enterprise's promise morphs into a financial focus and monetization. Pressures to commoditize customers increase. The bigger the enterprise gets, the greater the pressure.

Corinthian Colleges is a poster child for what can go wrong when an enrichment enterprise is for-profit and publicly traded. In June 2014, Corinthian Colleges, a publicly traded, for-profit higher education company that enrolls 72,000 students at over 100 campuses nationwide, announced its imminent bankruptcy. It was one of the largest higher education collapses in American history.

Corinthian Colleges was audited by the federal government and the results were that 50 percent of its programs were deemed to be either failing or in a "warning zone": 162 programs failed, more than any other for-profit college. Corinthian created its own private student loan system (which the company was lawfully allowed to do), despite knowing that most of the students would default. It did this because by law, no more than 90 percent of the company's revenues could come from federal financial aid. That meant that every dollar that Corinthian lent directly to students allowed it to receive an additional nine dollars in federal aid, making the loans profitable even with default rates of 50 percent or more. At its peak, Corinthian received more than half a billion dollars per year from the federal Pell Grant program, more than the entire University of California system. Two-thirds of Corinthian students dropped out, about half of them within three months of enrolling.

For enrichment enterprises, it's better to opt out of the public market and create a privately held enterprise. Private investors and carefully managed loans can take the place of capital provided by stock sales and avoid the pressures to continually increase revenue and monetize what shouldn't be monetized.

The Right Culture for an Enrichment Enterprise and How Fifteen Cultural Drivers Must Be Practiced

The enrichment customer promise requires a cultivation culture. This culture's central focus is *value-centered goal attainment.* The culture builds from there, emphasizing the connection between values and actions.

The enrichment enterprise is a possibility-personal enterprise. It pays attention chiefly to potentiality, ideals and beliefs, values, aspirations and inspirations, and creative options. Its decision-making is people driven, organic, open-minded, and subjective. Decision-making is fundamentally based on *people's judgment.*

The hardest decision in most enrichment enterprises is how to measure progress. If you are Habitat for Humanity, knowing whether or not you are succeeding is easy—homes are getting built or they are not. When you get to "development," "fulfillment of potential," or an "uplifting experience" at an opera, things get more complex. These kinds of values are worked with differently. Leaders and employees need to start with: When this value is realized what does it look like *in behavior*? They can, then, track progress by seeing to what extent these behaviors occur.

When it comes to "measuring" the "uplifting experience" of an opera, the only choice the director and performers have is to simply ask patrons if their experience was positive, negative, or somewhere in between. Operas can get valuable information from return visits from patrons, season-ticket holders signing up year after year, and reviews. But, trying to measure the inner experience(s) of patrons is difficult. At a day care center it's even harder. Leaders and teachers first need to decide what "development" means. Is it physical development, cognitive development, social development, learning certain kinds of information, activity level, attention span, and communication skills? Next, they need to come up with behaviors that directly or indirectly indicate that actual development has occurred.

For example, if leaders and teachers conclude that communication skills are crucial, they need to describe what communication skill development looks like in behavior. When they have accomplished this, they have the measures of progress that they need. This kind of thing is as close to verifiability as a day care center can get, and once they have articulated their measures, they can use them to lead and manage performance.

The important point here is that the enrichment enterprise's performance is essentially a matter of *people judgment.* There is no data-based, objective, or fact-based way to measure progress. The two impersonal decision-making enterprises—predictable and dependable and best-in-class—can use data and facts, but the two personal decision-making enterprises—customized and enrichment—cannot, or should not! This distinction has major implications, which will be discussed more in Chapter 9.

Not understanding this distinction between personal and impersonal decision-making is a major cause of Kids First's difficulties described earlier. The central power of a day care center is *will or belief power.* Parents enroll their children because they *believe in* furthering the development and enrichment of their children. Teachers and caretakers work there because they believe in the same thing. Enabling the full and successful expression of this kind of power is the basis for the center's success. Diminishing this power guarantees failure. It's like trying to build a car company by selling cars without engines.

Making monetization a day care center's purpose completely changes the power dynamic. It puts hierarchical power front and center, which pulls each center into a control culture. The control culture—perfect for a predictable and dependable enterprise—is the exact opposite of what a cultivation culture needs. A control culture introduces major crosscurrents into each center. Day in and day out, teachers and caretakers (the "engines" of the enterprise) are being pulled in two, diametrically opposed, directions.

Kids First's leaders are unconsciously creating conditions that influence everything that happens in each center and ultimately ensures their enterprise's failure. Decision-making should be based on the values that parents (and their children) and teachers hold dear. People's judgment should be the basis for decision-making, not data-based profitability. Profitability in a day care center depends on the quality and effectiveness of the teachers' decisions, judgment, and care. Introducing a control culture that makes decisions based on monetization impedes the teachers' judgment and wears them out. Teachers care for the children every day *in spite of* the forces impinging on them. When decisions become based on monetization, the criteria for rewarding teachers become contradictory, and day-to-day operations in the new control culture create more and more unresolved conflicts.

Managing conflict is probably more difficult for an enrichment enterprise than for any of the other three, because the mind-set of this enterprise is based on *intentionality*. When conflict emerges, people easily slip into questioning the intentions of those voicing conflicting opinions. Too much of this causes people to stop voicing disagreement, and when this is taken to an extreme, people are slow to realize that the enterprise is in trouble. Understanding this tendency in enrichment enterprises and establishing a norm of "agreeing to disagree" is the most effective way to manage conflict.

The architecture of an enrichment enterprise (structure, hiring, nature of work, pay, teaming, and use of information technology) is based on whatever people decide will most effectively bring about the realization of the enterprise's values. You could call this organized freedom.

Developing children, for example, calls for considerable cooperation, sharing of ideas, and teachers helping one another out. Judging the extent to which each unique child is developing calls for considerable co-judgment among teachers. It also calls for a very flat organization, free access to everyone involved, and freedom of self-expression. This means that at Kids First, for example, the organizational structure at each center should be open, circular, and malleable (easily changed). A hierarchy stifles connections within the center that need to be horizontal, not vertical. Each center should be one big team, not one teacher assigned to a classroom, each kept behind a closed door. New teachers should be hired by other teachers, not people with imposing titles positioned above the teachers. Pay should be essentially tied to how well the children are developing, how satisfied parents are, and how well each center is growing because of positive recommendations from parents. Information technology provides the basics and access to new concepts and new methods regarding the development and care of children.

Enrichment retailers, like The Body Shop, Tom's Shoes, or Patagonia are rare. But these retailers would be structured like most brick-and-mortar retail stores (which are predictable and dependable enterprises), though with more freedom for judgment-making, experimentation, and customer interaction at the local level. Treatment and treatment-related enterprises would vary in architecture—some might be in an office park or shopping center, others might be standalone entities. More often than not, the arts take place in a large arts center.

Innovation, training (particularly "on-the-job" training), and change are an ongoing part of the enrichment enterprise's cultivation culture. Its people are naturally motivated to keep trying to do things better. The enrichment enterprise is more open to change and development than any of the three other enterprises, and needs to remain open, so creative and innovative ideas can be continually voiced and heard.

The Right Leadership for an Enrichment Enterprise and How Three Leadership Drivers Must Be Practiced

The right leadership for an enrichment enterprise is charismatic. The literal definition of charismatic is to "breathe life into." This phrase captures the essence of this leadership approach: to enliven others, to catalyze growth, to fulfill potential for customers and employees. A charismatic leader energizes people and creates conditions within the organization so that the enterprise's values can be realized. The charismatic leader is a steward. He or she energizes people and encourages them to actively participate in the enterprise's efforts to realize its values and beliefs.

Let's go back to Kids First. The viability and success of this enterprise is rooted in how well its teachers care for and develop the children. It will prosper only if it profitably delivers on its promise to its customers. The leader of the center has to create the conditions necessary for that to happen and recognize that it all depends on the teachers' judgment and behavior. The shareholders' prosperity depends on how well the teachers develop the children under their care. The leader of the center needs to *enable* that development; it cannot be controlled from on high. This means that the center has to grow organically; the center's growth cannot be mandated any more than a tomato's growth can. It has to be germinated and cultivated.

The center's leader needs to clarify the center's values and work with the teachers to determine what those values look like in behavior. Decisions about how to develop the children under their care are made principally by the teachers. A leader centers his or her behavior on empowering the teachers to deliver on their promise of enrichment. He or she then works with the teachers to set goals, monitor the attainment of those goals, and help the teachers be as effective as they can be. He or she celebrates success all along the way and treats the teachers as co-leaders and co-problem-solvers.

Charismatic leaders emphasize getting people dedicated to a common vision. They foster people's commitment. They believe that people will dedicate themselves to doing their best if they are committed to the enrichment purpose of the organization and are given an opportunity to grow and develop.

Charismatic leaders encourage creativity and new ideas. They are open to change. They are enthusiastic, positive, and insightful. They typically create a lively, spontaneous, and magnetic organization where people feel like there is never a dull moment. They welcome self-expression. They strive to capture the imagination of their people and inspire allegiance to the mission of the enterprise. They understand that willpower drives the enterprise and that energy comes from commitment to its values.

Stewart Hansen is a Presbyterian minister in the heart of oil country; most of his session (board) members are oil company executives. He is magnetic and has single-handedly grown his church's membership. At a meeting with his fellow ministers, he said: "The session keeps asking me to design and implement a system for managing all of you. They want me to build job descriptions for each of you and establish more rules and policies. I know they have the church's best interests at heart, but I am having a hard time agreeing with what they are telling me to do and I am not sure why. I am in quite a quandary. I could use your help thinking this through."

Stewart's struggle is like Kids First's teachers' struggle. The oil executives in the session are trying to help Stewart lead his fellow ministers, but their suggestions contradict the church's mission—or that of any enrichment enterprise. The executives are telling Stewart that the way to manage the performance of his ministers is to do it the way that they do it in their respective oil companies.

How you manage performance in an oil company, which is a predictable and dependable enterprise, is the exact opposite of how you manage performance in a church. These kinds of well-intentioned disconnections go on all the time, in every enterprise. The three drivers of leadership in any enterprise are to set direction, to mobilize commitment, and to build organizational capability. In an enrichment enterprise, leaders set direction by establishing and clarifying the values that their enterprise believes in and intends to realize. They then build a plan with their people that provides a roadmap for how to do that.

Charismatic leaders put a great deal of energy into mentoring and counseling their employees. They emphasize helping their people grow, develop, and succeed. Teaching comes naturally to them. They mobilize commitment by involving their people and co-determining with them what each accomplished goal looks like in behavior. They work with their people to establish how everyone will know when the values they espouse have been realized. Leaders and their people build plans to accomplish each goal. Then they meet regularly to track how people are progressing and where they need to do something different. They celebrate successes all along the way. They create a culture that focuses on what is working and not working, define failure simply as negative feedback, and emphasize what it will take to get the enterprise back on track. They ensure that everyone stays close to the enterprise's customers and continue to elicit feedback from customers about what is working and not working. Importantly, they celebrate accomplishments, encourage people, and work to keep people focused on how to make things work.

They build organizational capability by hiring people who fit their customer promise and culture, actively developing people, staying open to new ideas and methods, and fostering inclusion. They keep looking at how to structure work in ways that most enable people to accomplish the goals of the enterprise. They are careful to keep resources allocated to the core of the enterprise that is directly responsible for delivering on the enterprise's customer promise. They keep administrative costs down as much as they can. They ensure that support groups operate in service to the core.

Yvon Chouinard, Patagonia's founder and CEO, is a classic example of a charismatic leader. From day one, he articulated the company's values and ensured that they guided everything that the company did. He was inspirational. People followed him because they believed in what Patagonia stood for. He built a culture that continually reinforced the company's environmental ethics.

He regularly reminded his employees that Patagonia's success hinged on them working well together. He encouraged his people to come up with as many ideas as they could about how the company could do things better. He fostered adaptation and openness to change. He was empathic with his employees and always fostered their growth and development. He spent time with his employees and worked with them to discover and utilize their strengths.

He was a continual source of optimism and enthusiasm. He regularly reminded people that "blaming will get you nowhere." His approach was always one of how do we get things to work and "can do." Not surprisingly, Patagonia has been a success since it opened in 1970.

The major strengths of the enrichment enterprise are its:

- Ability to build commitment and dedication among its people
- Openness and creativity
- Natural interest in change and development
- Freedom
- Encouragement of self-expression

Its major weaknesses are that it can:

- Lose direction and focus
- Take on too much and get overcommitted
- Tend to sweep problems under the rug
- Be averse to anything that smacks of control
- Be reluctant to hold people accountable

Many are reluctant to recognize the legitimacy of the enrichment enterprise because of its inherent subjectivity—that baffles some people. They aren't sure how to deal with it. How do you lead, manage, decide, organize, etc. an enterprise that is centered on the realization of values? How do you hold people accountable in this enterprise? How should it be measured? This confusion is perfectly natural, but the way many people deal with it is to try to keep the enterprise under control—especially when profit demands, stock prices, shareholders, and public market expectations are involved. Thus, those who don't understand enrichment enterprises tend to treat them as predictable and dependable enterprises.

This is particularly unfortunate because the predictable and dependable enterprise is antithetical to an enrichment enterprise. Of course, the enrichment enterprise needs to be managed just as every other enterprise needs to be managed. However, because the question of how to manage an enrichment enterprise is difficult for some people, they, again understandably, default to central control, hierarchy, policies and procedures, etc. They try to come up with "hard" data, verifiable evidence, formulas, and prescriptions. While some parts of enrichment enterprises can and should be managed and measured this way, the simple truth is that most of these enterprises are best managed by people making *judgments*.

Almost any enrichment enterprise is a quintessential grassroots undertaking. Its very existence springs from goodwill, values, and beliefs. It is rooted in "people possibilities." It evolves. It is organic. Its power comes from "willed"-power. Change goes with the territory. Most enrichment enterprises have no limits, no end points. There is always more that can be done.

Predictable and dependable enterprises are premised on the exact opposite—and those in charge try to engineer things so that change does not occur. They build structures that keep processes in control and keep necessary limits in place. Power is based on title so there is always someone in control.

But an enrichment enterprise is an endeavor to continually fulfill people's potential. It warms the hearts of its customers. You can see its benefits in the faces of its customers. The enrichment enterprise is more idealistic than the other types. It focuses on helping its customers transcend. More often than not, it is about hope.

Charismatic leaders put considerable faith in the willfulness and goodwill of their people. They understand that they and their people are "co-believers" and that their job is to encourage and foster the realization of those beliefs.

4

THE BEST-IN-CLASS ENTERPRISE

Creating and Delivering Distinctive
Products and Services

➤ ➤ ➤

Steve Jobs, Apple's CEO, asked Scott Forstall to meet with him and to keep the meeting secret. Forstall was a team leader and brilliant engineer. Jobs told him that the company was starting a new project, called "Project Purple," that it was "top secret," and that he wanted Forstall to build and lead the team of engineers who could do it best. Forstall wasn't to recruit anyone from outside, nor could he tell the team what the project was about.

Forstall went around the company looking for superstar engineers in different parts of the company, telling them only what he'd been allowed to tell them, and adding, "I can't tell you who you will work for. What I can tell you is that, if you accept this project, you will work nights, weekends, probably for a number of years."

The Project Purple team took over an entire building at Apple's Cupertino, California, headquarters. Only they were allowed into the building. They were told not to talk to anyone outside of the building about the project. Then they broke down into two separate but closely integrated groups—the software group and the hardware group. Each was composed of carefully selected kinds of engineering expertise. Innumerable prototypes were created and tested to make sure that parts of software and hardware actually worked. One hardware button went through fifty refinements. Every component of the product was subject to externally based verification (i.e., facts, proven formulas, objective tests). One of Apple's designers described the company's endeavor as "imagining products that don't exist and guiding them to life."

Project Purple took four years to develop the iPhone.

Welcome to the world of best-in-class enterprises. This enterprise is premised on the notion that its customers are paying for products or services that are distinctive and unique. They promise to deliver the best product and/or service, period. Like the iPhone, the product or service is conceptualized from within the enterprise and creates its own market. The enterprise is driven by expertise; most of its leaders are usually experts.

The iPhone did not come about because one customer called Apple and asked for a customized smartphone—that's what would have happened if Apple were a customized enterprise. It was "imagined" and "guided to life" by Apple. Apple did not invent the smartphone. That distinction belongs to IBM, which came up with the IBM Simon in 1994. What Apple did was take the smartphone to a whole different level of functionality and capability. And, almost single-handedly, the iPhone has taken Apple to a market capitalization of $524 billion and made it one of the top three most valuable companies in the world.

It is not hard to see why Apple is, and has been, so secretive about what it is up to. The smartphone market is extremely lucrative and extremely competitive. In the high-tech sector you can be in business on Monday and out of business on Tuesday—all it takes is for one of your competitors to come up with a significantly better product that makes yours obsolete overnight. High-tech companies cannot let competitors get wind of what they are up to when it comes to product development. It is also not hard to see why superior expertise is so important. Apple's central viability depends upon the competency of its array of experts.

In a free-market economy every enterprise engages in competition, but if you want to work in the most highly competitive enterprise possible, join a best-in-class enterprise.

IN THIS CHAPTER, READERS WILL LEARN:

- How exactly customers need to be approached in this kind of enterprise
- The right culture for a best-in-class enterprise

- How fifteen culture drivers (decision-making, hiring, performance management, compensation, and eleven more) need to be practiced
- The right leadership approach for a best-in-class enterprise
- How three leadership drivers need to be practiced

The Best-In-Class Enterprise Customer Promise and How It Must Approach Its Customers

Mark's proprietary approach to options trading and investments plus Don's marketing expertise made them the perfect partners for a new options-trading investment service—or so they thought. Mark had spent fifteen years developing and testing his trading system, and it was ready to present to the marketplace. Don was a marketing whiz and had a sterling track record in generating revenues for several major companies.

Mark and Don started their trading company by offering a recommended daily trade based on Mark's proprietary system. All that customers needed to do was to open their own options-trading account with any broker that they chose, and then follow the system's recommendation. Customers quickly multiplied, and it didn't take long before their company was beating the competition and doing well financially. Five years later, they had twenty-five employees and a solid customer base.

Then Mark and Don started arguing nonstop. Mark was focused on improving his sophisticated trading method and Don was focused on developing a systematic and structured marketing and sales campaign. Mark and Don clashed on every issue; each thought the other's stubbornness was the problem. They tried to get along—until Don insisted that Mark take his proprietary options-trading system, publish it in an ebook, and put it up for sale. Mark strongly disagreed. Mark's view was that making his system available to the general public would commoditize it and give away the company's distinct competitive advantage in the marketplace. Don's belief was that making the system available to all via ebook sales would significantly reduce their costs and expand their market at the same time. They decided to part ways. Mark stayed with the company and Don took a marketing position with another company.

Mark's and Don's approaches were each legitimate—separately. But, together, they didn't work. Mark's mind-set fit the company's customer promise—to be a best-in-class investment service. Don's did not: He took a predictable and dependable approach.

In a best-in-class enterprise, customers are paying for products and/or services that are distinctive and unmatched. Mark's proprietary trading system was one-of-a-kind, and it was much more effective than the competition's offerings. Customers paid for Mark's system because it worked, it was the best system available, and no one else had it.

Unaware of the four enterprise types, Don did not understand that his idea would pull the company apart, turn it into a mass-market training-product company, and take it out of the trading business. Mark's trading system would have to be homogenized and commoditized in order for a wide spate of readers to understand it. Commoditizing the system made the company into a predictable and dependable enterprise. Don's idea is a perfectly legitimate idea, and the predictable and dependable enterprise is equally legitimate. The problem is that the two enterprises are fundamentally different from one another—their customer promises are different, their cultures are different, and their leadership approaches are different.

So the cause of Mark's and Don's conflict was not their personalities— it was the fact that the two enterprises are fundamentally different from one another and could not have co-existed. If Mark and Don had tried to lead and operate their company as both a best-in-class and predictable and dependable enterprise, each of the two enterprises would have spent every day canceling one another out.

The best-in-class enterprise promises excellence. Its product or service is highly desirable and unparalleled. Tiffany & Company's *Blue Book* catalog was first published in 1845. The *Blue Book* is the company's catalogue of "flawless craftsmanship and peerless design which heralds the fall season with one of the most extensive and exquisite collections of couture jewelry on earth. These breathtaking masterpieces of exceedingly rare gems are eagerly anticipated by the world's jewelry connoisseurs who flock to Tiffany to be the first to see and buy these one-of-a-kind treasures."

The best-in-class enterprise provides products and/or services that continually redefine the state of the art and are based on unique technology or know-how. In 1959, Xerox introduced the first plain paper copier, named the Xerox 914. It was an instant hit. Two years later, it had generated almost $60 million in revenue. By 1965, it was generating $500 million in revenue. Today, the name Xerox is equated with the copier—now, when someone wants to make a copy of something, they "Xerox" it.

What sets the best-in-class enterprise apart from the other three enterprises is its in-house innovation. A true best-in-class enterprise creates its own market. Masaru Ibuka, co-founder of Sony, Inc., wanted to be able to listen to operas during his frequent trans-Pacific plane trips. Sony had invented the transistor radio in 1955, which allowed people to listen to the radio in different locations. Ibuka wondered if Sony could invent a device that allowed people to listen to pre-recorded music on the move. He asked his engineers to see what they could do. One year later, Sony introduced the Walkman. First released in Japan, it was a massive hit. Sony sold over 50,000 of them in the first two months. Over the next two decades, the company sold over 400 million around the globe. A whole new market for portable, personal, and private (using headphones) listening to music emerged.

Bell Laboratories is another example. Since its founding, it has produced thousands of scientific and engineering innovations, many of which have led to the creation of major markets. These inventions include (among others): the electrical-relay digital computer, the transistor, the telephone switching system, satellite communications, sonar, lasers, and solar cells. No customer even imagined any of them.

What also sets this enterprise type apart from the other three is the salience of expertise. Expertise is at its center. Best-in-class enterprises are always highly talent-intensive. The message here is not that the best-in-class enterprise is the only kind of enterprise that utilizes expertise. Expertise plays a role in all four enterprises, but it is the central driving force for a best-in-class enterprise. Expertise plays a supporting role in the other three enterprises—it is channeled into their particular central requirements. In the customized enterprise, expertise is used as needed to provide a customized solution for each unique customer. In a predictable and dependable enterprise, expertise is channeled into what operational functions (e.g., power generation or transmission) need in order to effectively perform. In an enrichment enterprise, expertise is used to whatever extent it is needed in order to realize a particular value or belief. But expertise plays only a supporting role in enrichment, predictable and dependable, and customized enterprises. In a best-in-class enterprise, experts *are* the enterprise. They come up with the products themselves—they are the ones who deliver the customer promise. They come up with the concepts for product or services (e.g., the iPhone) and then rely on the right set of talented experts to realize ("guide to life") that concept. If a best-in-class enterprise does not have *the best* expertise, it will fail. Leaders in this type of enterprise make a big mistake if they take their experts for granted. If they do, their enterprise will fail.

Not surprisingly, another characteristic of the best-in-class enterprise is that its products or services are the most expensive. Some are rare and in short supply; others are one-of-a-kind. If you have created or own the "best," if there is only one and you have it, you can put a high price on it. The Ty Warner Penthouse Suite at the Four Seasons Hotel in New York goes for $41,836 per night. A one-of-a-kind Tiffany necklace can set you back $20,000 and up. A Lamborghini Veneno will cost you $4.6 million.

If you could put all of the leaders and employees from all of the best-in-class enterprises in a room and ask them how they really want to approach their customers, they would say that they want customers to come to them. If they had their druthers, they would simply make it known that their product or service was available, and then watch people line up at their doors. And, in the most successful best-in-class enterprises, this is what happens. When Apple advertised that the new 6S iPhone would be in stores, thousands of people lined up outside to buy it. Some even camped out overnight so that they could buy one before the store ran out. This preference for customer approach is not hard to understand. It would be incongruent for the experts who conceptualized and created a one-of-a-kind product or service to want to convince people that they should buy it. Their reasoning is like Apple's: the first iPhone took four years to create. It is the best smartphone available on the market. No one else has anything like it. Why on earth should I have to *sell* it?

Customers come calling to Apple, Tiffany & Company, Intel, or Four Seasons Hotels. A best-in-class start-up or unknown has to get the word out and sell. The more it delivers on its customer promise, the less selling it will have to do. If there is an enterprise that has a product or service that "sells itself," it is the best-in-class enterprise.

For high-tech best-in-class enterprises, like Apple and Google, customers very often need to be educated on how much the product or service can do and what it takes to get its full benefit. So, best-in-class enterprises need to be ready to work with their customers to provide that education. Apple's "Genius Bar" is a clear example of this.

In business-to-business sales, it is very often necessary for a best-in-class enterprise to bring appropriate experts into the selling process. Prospective customers typically have their own experts present in sales meetings. Salespeople need to step aside and let the experts talk with one another. Thermo Fisher Scientific, Inc., describes itself as the "world leader in serving science." This best-in-class enterprise "helps customers accelerate life sciences research, solve complex analytical challenges, improve patient diagnostics and increase laboratory productivity." Thermo Fisher Scientific salespeople always bring the appropriate company expert with them to sales meetings, and their prospective customers do the same with their experts. The company sells such products as mass spectrometry, PCR enzymes, master mixes, and GeneArt Gene Synthesis. Expert-to-expert conversations are critical to the sale.

Each of the four enterprises can take things too far and upset their customers. Enterprises opposite to one another on the attention and decision-making axes mistreat their customers in mirror opposite ways. The predictable and dependable enterprise can take its customers for granted. The enrichment enterprise can take its intentions too far and slip into making promises that it can't live up to. The customized enterprise can get too chummy with its customers and refrain from voicing a different opinion about what will work best for them. The best-in-class enterprise can treat customers arrogantly.

Law firms are typically best-in-class enterprises. Their customer promise is superior legal expertise. To a large extent, customers of a law firm are in the dark because they don't know the law. So, they are in a highly dependent position with their lawyer. The practice of law is stressful, demanding, complicated, and pressured. Lawyers have to be "right." They have to "win." People are angry. If you would like a template for the likelihood of arrogant behavior, lawyering is a good place to start. This is not meant as a criticism. It is a simple statement of probability, not inevitability. The stage is set for a law firm to behave arrogantly. The BTI Consulting Group issues an annual ranking of the "most arrogant" U.S. law firms.

Prices vary more in best-in-class enterprises than in other types. They range from $55 for a Nike shoe to $55 million for the Mouawad 637-carat L'Incomparable diamond necklace. The more rare, exquisite, and desirable the item, the higher the price. Needless to say, pricing can get quite complicated in this enterprise. The number of possible buyers varies widely. It's in the millions for Nike shoes and perhaps only one for the Mouawad necklace.

Planning and budgeting can get equally complicated. At this point, Nike probably has developed reliable formulas for revenues, costs, markets, inventory, shipping, warehousing, etc. and can build plans each year with reasonable certainty. It is hard to imagine what a plan might look like regarding the Mouawad necklace. By now, Nike probably takes last year's budget, the coming year's plan, and re-budgets from there. Budgeting for the sale of the necklace is likely a non sequitur. Given the central importance of expertise in this enterprise, experts play a much bigger role in pricing, planning, and budgeting than they do in the other three enterprises.

The Right Culture for a Best-In-Class Enterprise and How Fifteen Cultural Drivers Must Be Practiced

At the Research In Motion, Ltd. (RIM), board meeting in late 2012 CEO Thorsten Heins presented plans for the launch of a new phone designed to turn around the company's fortunes. RIM's major success, the keyboard-equipped BlackBerry phone, was losing the battle against Apple's (and others') touchscreen phone. According to Heins, the BlackBerry Z10 smartphone (also keyboard-equipped) was the solution to the company's major problems. But, one of the company's directors had a problem. "RIM has a cultural problem and the Z10 is an example of it," he said. The director was Michael Lazaridis, the engineer behind the BlackBerry, the company's co-founder, and its former co-CEO. Lazaridis said that he had recently met with several senior executives and they had told him that "the market for keyboard-equipped mobile phones was dead." Lazaridis believed that the touchscreen phone was a passing fancy and that RIM's keyboard-equipped smartphone would prevail, but the major dissension within the company's senior executive ranks was destroying the company.

At the time of this board meeting, RIM, once the giant of the smartphone business, was in big trouble. It had just reported a $965 million second-quarter loss, primarily because of a huge write-down of Z10 phones that no one was buying. RIM had somehow managed to lose its runaway lead and become a bit player in the smartphone market it invented. In addition, there were deep rifts at the executive and boardroom levels.

RIM (now re-named BlackBerry, Ltd.) had grown to become a hierarchical, multilayered behemoth and top-down-controlled enterprise. Marketing and Finance held sway in the company. Lazaridis and Jim

Balsillie, the other co-founder of the company and a marketer, publicly belittled the iPhone (which had emerged as the market leader) and its shortcomings. "That's what marketing is all about," Balsillie explained. In its attempt to compete with Apple and others, including Google and Motorola, RIM bought Torch Mobile, a software development firm that created Internet browsers for mobile phones. Senior executives demanded that RIM engineers incorporate Torch Mobile's software into the BlackBerry, but the process proved too complex and too time-consuming. It bought QNX software and required that engineers change the phone's operating system to the one built by QNX. That meant that a new team of engineers from QNX would, essentially, recreate the BlackBerry. This QNX team clashed with the company's existing engineers, which pushed decision-making up the company's hierarchy. Discussions among the senior leaders dragged on for a year.

One engineer noted that the company was paying attention to what customers were doing, but "we believed we knew better what customers needed long term than they did." As the company grew into a $20 billion enterprise, the new hierarchical structure made it difficult to get definitive decisions or establish clear accountability. This caused the company to always be slow to market. Feedback from customers that indicated that the BlackBerry needed to be something different died at middle management, because senior executives did not want to add more internal battles to those that already existed. New ideas from engineering were dismissed because senior executives did not want to confuse the marketing message already in place. Senior executives would make a decision, but executives below them would actively work to sabotage the decision.

Michael Lazaridis was right. RIM did have a cultural problem. What he thought was causing the cultural problem (the dissension within the company's senior ranks) was a symptom of a deeper problem. RIM had morphed into a culture (and leadership approach) that fit with a predictable and dependable enterprise but did not fit with a best-in-class enterprise. RIM was, and still is, a best-in-class enterprise. At a fundamental level, the company had unknowingly replaced expertise power (which fits a best-in-class enterprise) with role (titular) power (which fits a predictable and dependable enterprise). This is not unusual. The same thing has happened with Microsoft, Kodak, and many other companies. Microsoft appears to have overcome this problem—by turning leadership over to an engineer (expert). Kodak is still trying to recover. The pressure on a big, highly successful best-in-class enterprise to morph into a predictable and dependable enterprise is immense. It is human nature to default to control when you have 50,000 employees! However, when that happens, the nature and use of *power* changes and this change has major consequences. Quite a number of cultural and leadership factors change as well, but the centrally important change is the power change.

The root cause of RIM's success was engineering expertise, not marketing and not finance. Engineering expertise *powers* the company. Marketing and finance are important, but, at the end of the day, RIM will succeed or fail by the quality and effectiveness of its engineering expertise. Given customers' preference for the iPhone, the only way for RIM to succeed is to come up with a smartphone that does everything the iPhone does and more, or to design and manufacture something entirely different that takes the smartphone market to a whole different level—and that can happen only with experts in power.

In a best-in-class enterprise, someone's title really has nothing to do with success. Expertise gets you where you want to go and expertise keeps you there. The only way RIM will keep itself from failing is to "out-engineer" the competition and to fully rely on the feedback received from customers (i.e., sales). In a best-in-class enterprise, the product or service really does sell itself. That was true when the BlackBerry was selling like hotcakes, and it was still true when people stopped buying it. Why would you listen to positive feedback from your customers on the way up (i.e., sales) but ignore negative feedback from your customers on the way down (i.e., no sales)?

As the nature and use of power changed at RIM, so did its structure (from matrix/adhocracy [task teams that accomplish a particular result and then disband] to hierarchy), decision-making (from customer feedback regarding the product to the thinking of someone with an important title), and management of conflict (from customers' buying behavior to a high-level executive's conclusion). Acquisitions (Torch Mobile and QNX) were made before everyone was clear on what kind of product the company needed to engineer in order to outdistance the competition. Marketing and Finance behaved as if they needed to hold sway instead of operating in service to engineering and manufacturing.

The kind of culture that fits a best-in-class enterprise is the competence culture, which is centered on pursuing excellence. It demands the highest level of capability and expertise possible and continually works to capitalize on that expertise. It is very often a meritocracy because some experts are much more competent than others or possess a critical kind of expertise that is very hard to find. Innovation and creativity are the engine of this enterprise. Products and services are imagined and created from whole cloth here.

Because it is so competitive, this culture is not for the faint of heart. Every enterprise has to compete and needs competent people. The competence culture is predominantly competitive and filled with high achievers. It is intense and relentless. "Stretch" goals are routine. People are constantly challenged to do something better or take what they're doing to the next level. When Andy Grove, the long-time CEO of Intel (a best-in-class enterprise), says "only the paranoid survive," he means that in the best-in-class world you have to continually be looking over your shoulder to see what your competition is doing. When you join a best-in-class enterprise, you are choosing to be part of an undertaking that could be in business on one day and out of business the next. Apple out-engineered RIM and RIM "lost." Digital photography came along and put Kodak out of the film business. The Internet showed up and severely diminished the print Yellow Pages and World Encyclopedia. Only doctors and lawyers use fax machines today—fax machines have gone away thanks to e-mail, e-signature services, and scanners. The intensity of a best-in-class enterprise is caused by a mixture of excitement (of realizing a new concept) and fear (that one of your competitors will beat you to it). So here, people routinely work eighty hours a week. In its early days, Apple even had a T-shirt for employees that said "Working 100 hours a week and loving it."

Standards are very high in this culture. People are in a hurry. It is a win-lose atmosphere. High levels of competence (expertise) underpin success. If you choose to be the best at something, then you need the best people. Excellence is key. Issy Sharpe, the former chairman and CEO of Four Seasons Hotels, personally oversaw much of the interior design of new hotels on the drawing board. The hotels themselves are works of art. The best hoteliers and chefs in the world are hired. Every detail is attended to. Executives dedicate great attention and energy to developing services that are unique in the hotel industry. The company now has its own private jet and will fly you to the Four Seasons Hotel of your choice, anywhere in the world.

Given that the customized enterprise is the opposite enterprise to best-in-class and has a collaborative culture, you can expect the best-in-class enterprise to struggle with teaming. Breakups occur in law firms, consulting firms filled with experts, and high-tech start-ups much more frequently than in other kinds of enterprises.

Given its combination of attending to possibilities and deciding by impersonal means, the best-in-class enterprise's culture is centrally preoccupied with *verifiable conceptual goal attainment*. Xerox conceptualized a copier. But, before offering its actual copier in the marketplace, the company had to verify that it worked and that verification was data and fact based. It was not based on someone's opinion. It had a scientific cast to it. Apple's Project Purple team built a huge number of prototypes and conducted a great many experimental tests of the phone's hardware and software. As Microsoft developed its operating system software, it built the software during the day and tried to crash it every night.

In a best-in-class enterprise, small, medium, and large concepts of what might be are put to the test every step of the way. This culture takes nothing for granted. Talk is cheap. Everyone is from Missouri, the "show me" state. Performance has to be demonstrated and proved. Analytical capability often overshadows interpersonal capability. This culture has to verify its progress, using factual data, every step of the way.

This culture is not a good fit for interpersonally fragile people or people who take things personally. Steve Jobs definitely took things too far (got way out of balance), but he was the quintessential leader for this enterprise. It can get pretty brutal. It is all about "being right" and proving everything. Conflict is automatic in this culture. In fact, this enterprise needs conflict to succeed in the marketplace. But, it is "trial and error" conflict. In its purest sense, promotion is a misnomer in this culture. Competence in a given field matters most, not "moving up." Ideally, group and team leaders in this culture have a thorough understanding of the kind of expertise needed and how to help different kinds of experts work together.

The organizational structure is matrix based (experts and project managers linked together) or an adhocracy. Project teams are the most common. Project Purple teams were formed with a particular set of experts to accomplish designing a workable component for the iPhone. This team was "projectized"—meaning that it had a project leader whose job it was to help the project reach milestones in an established amount of time. When the goal of a project was attained, the team disbanded. The decider was not someone with a title; it was the demonstrated and verified accomplishment of a particular goal.

Organizational structure was one of the main places where RIM went astray. When the iPhone appeared on the scene, RIM should have come up with its concept of a competitive smartphone and hired the necessary experts to design and build it. If the company was unable to conceptualize a competitive smartphone, then it could have explored going into an ancillary business or simply shut the company down and done something completely different with the profits on hand. The main point here is that letting executives with lofty titles make decisions made things worse for RIM.

In a best-in-class company, experts are hired by the expert teams and project managers. The candidate with the right expertise, experience in a particular specialty, and best track record gets hired. Beyond a beginning base salary, incentive pay is put in place for teams and individuals. The better the product or service performs in the marketplace, the more money everyone makes. Information technology operates principally in service to product or service development and implementation. Teams are built to attain conceptual goals—all along the design and development process. Teams are composed of the experts necessary to achieve a particular goal. They are fluid, ad hoc, and together for a project and then disbanded.

Training is based on needed expertise, particularly regarding new developments in appropriate technical fields. Change is fully embraced by all. Things can change on a dime in this culture. When you include innovation as a form of change, openness to change becomes a major factor in this culture. People need to be receptive to positive and negative feedback in this culture.

The Right Leadership for a Best-In-Class Enterprise and How Three Leadership Drivers Must Be Practiced

In early 2011, Time Warner Inc. fired Jack Griffin, chief executive of the media company's Time Inc. publishing unit, after less than six months on the job. Time Warner's CEO, Jeff Bewkes, had come to the conclusion that Griffin's leadership "did not mesh with Time Inc. and Time Warner."

People familiar with what happened said that Griffin exhibited "imperious behavior" that didn't sit well with the ranks at Time Inc. For example, Griffin insisted that every magazine issue include a masthead and that his name be on top. This went against a long-standing tradition at the company of leaving it up to individual editors whether to run a masthead. Griffin regularly ordered people to be at 7:30 a.m. meetings, despite people's requests that they start later because these meetings were interfering with family demands. He also surrounded himself with outside consultants, whose advice he listened to, while ignoring the ideas of his own leadership team and staff. His explicit message to his people was that he was on a personal mission to reinvent Time Inc.'s business and culture by having people focus on turning Time Inc. into a number of businesses, but particularly a marketing services business. According to a senior Time Warner executive, Griffin's appointment was a "disconnect from the beginning."

While it is tempting to chalk this "disconnect" up to egocentricity on Griffin's part, there is a deeper problem going on with his approach to leadership. His leadership was top-down, which fits a predictable and dependable enterprise, not a best-in-class enterprise like Time Inc. Best-in-class enterprises need standard-setter leadership. Time Inc.'s success rested on the quality of its editorial content and the quality of its writing. Leadership in a best-in-class enterprise such as Time Inc. requires challenging your editors and journalists to utilize their expertise to the fullest extent possible. Griffin wanted Time Inc. to go beyond its roots as a magazine publisher and move into other kinds of businesses. Ordering editors and journalists to transform the magazine's business into anything other than magazine publishing was a prescription for failure.

Customer promise determines what leadership approach is needed. If a leader, particularly a CEO, is primarily inclined to take a directive approach as Griffin was, he or she would, ideally, take the reins in a predictable and dependable enterprise. If, instead, a leader joins a best-in-class enterprise, then that leader would need to adopt the leadership *behaviors* of a standard-setter leader.

This approach to leadership is essentially a matter of identifying challenges and then challenging others to be the best that they can be. It has to do with identifying a unique and distinctive concept for the enterprise and then creating the required conditions for that concept to be realized. People follow the standard-setter leader because they believe in being the best. Steve Jobs at Apple conceived the idea of the Macintosh computer, the iPod, the iPhone, and the iPad. Then, he brought in the best experts he could and challenged them to bring these ideas "to life." Bill Gates did the same thing at Microsoft.

Standard-setter leaders are motivated to gain distinction, achieve something important, and pioneer new concepts. They come up with new ideas and believe they are better at something than anyone else. They are very competitive. As Robert Swiggett, CEO of Kollmorgen, tells his employees, "we will be the first with the best." The values of Kollmorgen are: "the best team wins; continuous improvement; customers talk, we listen; innovation defines our future; we compete for shareholders." Seymour Cray claimed that he was "obsessed by a vision of technological achievement, scientific purity, and quality" and, then, set about developing the best supercomputer. One of his fellow leaders claimed that Cray Computer is "in the business of advancing the state of the art."

So, if you want to work in a best-in-class enterprise, be ready to work for someone obsessed. Standard-setter leaders strive for perfection and want their employees to do the same. They set exacting expectations. They are taskmasters. They want everything planned out in detail and they often want to pass judgment on every detail. They push the limits and have a very hard time accepting the message "it can't be done." For them, things can always be done—and then done better.

When Jobs and his team designed the original Macintosh, Jobs's challenge to the team was to make it "insanely great." He never brought up profits or shareholder value maximization. "Just specify the computer's abilities," he said. At his first retreat with the Macintosh team he told them to "not compromise." His belief was that making the product great was what mattered the most. In his view, if you built a great product, the profits would follow.

This issue of profits versus products was the basis for the clash between Jobs and John Sculley, the marketing genius whom Jobs recruited from PepsiCo. Jobs believed that Apple needed to do whatever it took to make the right product and that the products' quality would drive Apple's success and generate long-term profits. Sculley believed that expert marketing and a short-term profit (per se) focus would drive that success. After Sculley was ousted and Jobs returned to Apple, he shifted Apple's focus back to making innovative products. "My passion has been to build an enduring company where people were motivated to make great products. Everything else was secondary. Sure, it was great to make a profit, because that was what allowed you to make great products. But the products, not the profits, were the motivation."

There is no resting on laurels in best-in-class enterprises. Continuous innovation is a requirement for survival. Competitors are continually nipping at one's heels. Andy Grove, the former CEO of the best-in-class enterprise Intel, believed that smart actions lead to success, but success breeds complacency. Complacency breeds failure, so constant innovation is a necessity. Standard-setter leaders are always pushing employees to stay a step ahead, to keep pushing the limits. As of January 2016, Apple had approximately 20,000 patents and 10,000 pending patent applications.

Satya Nadella, who replaced Steve Ballmer as CEO of Microsoft, when asked to name his most important goal, replied that Microsoft had allowed itself to get too preoccupied with preserving the past (particularly its Windows operating system) and not doing much more to create its future. "The question is: How do we take the intellectual capital of 130,000 people and innovate where none of the category definitions of the past will matter? To me, that is perhaps the big culture change—recognizing innovation and fostering its growth. We have to own an innovation agenda. Longevity in this business is about being able to reinvent yourself or invent the future."

Standard-setter leaders of best-in-class enterprises create constant pressure to move ahead, demand efficiency, and want facts that back up opinions. Hard analysis must occur before sound decisions can be made. Good results do not just happen. They have to be thought through and carefully—at times obsessively!—well-planned. The best-in-class leader needs to insist on fact-based thinking and keep the pressure on to get things done right.

These leaders are, by nature, strategists and conceptual visionaries. They take the long-range view, look down the road, and strive to anticipate every contingency. Future possibilities are what count. The real excitement is in what lies ahead and what can be created that is better. Leaders of best-in-class enterprises instinctively emphasize incentives and differential rewards. They foster individual and group competition and are quick to spot people's unique capabilities and capitalize on them. They are always on the lookout for "A players."

Leaders in a best-in-class enterprise set direction by describing their visions for the best products or services possible and what they must be able to do for customers. They describe market patterns and the implications of those patterns for their products or services. They describe what the enterprise's competition has been able to accomplish and not accomplish, and they clarify what needs to be done to win the marketplace.

They mobilize commitment by telling employees that they are the best in the business and that they have the capability and expertise to realize concepts that no one else has ever been able to. They challenge employees to achieve unique and distinguished results. They recognize outstanding achievements and convince people that they are with a one-of-a-kind enterprise. They encourage people to come up with new ideas and methods. They continually celebrate accomplishments all along the way.

They build organizational capability by providing their experts with whatever they need to create those products or services. They find and hire the exact spectrum of experts needed to accomplish the results required. They set high standards and keep raising the bar. They create a competitive environment and foster continuous innovation.

The best-in-class enterprise is the world's greatest testament to the combination of human creativity and the power of free enterprise. Creativity and the dynamic of free enterprise are present in all four enterprises, but they shine most brightly in best-in-class enterprises. Here, knowledge is advanced, trends are set, new markets are created, and new opportunities emerge. Expertise, creativity, and innovation are the core of this enterprise and, when coupled with the opportunity inherent in free enterprise, worldwide changes occur. Where would we be without electricity, the cotton gin, paper and pen, the steam engine, airplanes, the telephone, computers, television, plastics, the automobile, the camera, radio, the Internet, the printing press, the light bulb? All of these products owe their existence to the experts who conceptualized and built them in best-in-class enterprises—sometimes at great personal cost to themselves.

This enterprise is also a particularly strong testament to the importance of creating conditions for the expression of the human spirit, free thinking, and knowing that we are contributing and winning. The four enterprises delineated in this book are not machines. They have machinelike characteristics (some more than others), but they are not machines. Machines did not create the iPhone or the Internet. They were created by innovative and spirited people who wanted to make a difference.

The best-in-class enterprise succeeds or fails by dint of the quality of its expertise. The clash between Jobs and Sculley at Apple brought this truism to the test. Jobs knew that Apple's products were the key to the company's success. He knew that the right products sold themselves and that the quality of Apple's expertise would make or break the company because that expertise created the products. Juiced-up marketing was not the key. Marketing was important, but it was not the key. Marketing needed to function *in service to* expertise, not vice versa. Expertise is at the core of the best-in-class enterprise. The core of the customized enterprise is a knowledgeable relationship (with each customer). The core of the enrichment enterprise is a deeply held value. And the core of the predictable and dependable enterprise is its operational system. In all four enterprises, everything outside the core needs to support and enhance that core. The core of each enterprise drives delivery on that enterprise's customer promise. In the best-in-class enterprise, expertise cannot be put in the backseat or in a sidecar. It has to continuously be in the driver's seat.

The best-in-class enterprise is a difficult enterprise to lead. It is filled with very bright experts, each of whom believes he or she is right, is very competitive, and is highly motivated to gain personal distinction. It is like herding cats. Leaders in this enterprise need to be experts in their own right. They need to be flexible and able to adapt to continually changing circumstances. They need to ensure that everyone understands the concept at hand and the plan for getting there. They need to be able to effectively deploy a wide range of experts. And, they need to lay out for people how everyone will make decisions. If how to decide is left open-ended, they get a lot of very smart people telling one another that they are right and everyone else is wrong. When this enterprise is product focused, it is usually a good idea to put project managers in place who can shepherd the *process* of product design and development.

The best-in-class enterprise is filled with tension. Tension, properly managed, is a key contributor to its success. Leaders need to be adept at fostering tension and re-framing it as necessary for success, but only to express it in a positive, constructive way.

If you are a leader in this kind of enterprise and your enterprise is highly successful, you would be highly advised to worry about that very success. Success in a best-in-class enterprise will, more often than not, pull you and your fellow leaders more and more into a predictable and dependable enterprise. This is quite understandable. The more successful you are, the more you don't want to lose or even risk your success. Parts of your enterprise will advise you—even pressure you—to keep things in control, but if you start using titles to make decisions about your experts, products, and services, you will jeopardize the very success you are trying to preserve. Let expertise continue to flourish and let hard data stay the basis for your decisions. The expertise that got you there is the same expertise that will keep you there.

5

THE CUSTOMIZED ENTERPRISE

Delivering a Tailored Solution for
Each Unique Customer

➤ ➤ ➤

A large grocery chain was worried about its shopping carts. Store managers were getting a lot of complaints from customers. The carts were unwieldy and unsafe. Babies were not secure enough in the seats (22,000 children in the United States are injured every year while in a shopping cart). On a downhill slope, loose carts reached 35 miles per hour. Carts got stolen a lot.

So the company called IDEO and asked it to design a shopping cart that would solve these problems. IDEO is a very successful design firm that tailors products to fit exactly what each unique customer needs. The company's website describes the firm's customer approach as "human-centered design." Human-centered design is "a creative approach to problem solving that starts with people and ends with innovative solutions that are tailor made to suit their needs."

In the case of the rogue shopping cart, IDEO put together a team of diverse thinkers to brainstorm and tackle the problem. The team was composed of an engineer, a Harvard MBA, a psychologist, an M.D., a linguist, a biologist, and a marketing expert. The team brainstormed ideas, came up with four prototypes, tested all four with real shoppers, took the results from the tests, came up with a cart that they thought solved the grocery chain's problem(s) and tested the "next-to-final" prototype again. They made a few revisions in the design and presented the final prototype to their customer.

The new shopping cart was exactly what the grocery chain needed.

IDEO has no titles in the company, no hierarchy, no policies and procedures manual, no departments. These are a fit with a predictable and dependable enterprise. IDEO just has many teams, each of which is composed of people from very diverse backgrounds. Each team has a facilitator who does nothing but guide the "people" process. When asked why the company does not have people with titles who are tiered up to the "top," IDEO's answer is that no one person could possibly come up with workable solutions that fit a plethora of different customers, each of whom had a unique need. The company describes its process as "focused chaos" and "enlightened trial and error." It welcomes failure because failure tells the team what is not working. The customer is the decider, not someone with an imposing title.

IDEO is a classic customized enterprise. In a customized enterprise customers are paying for a close, highly attentive, synergistic relationship and a product or service designed just for them. The enterprise partners with each unique customer, thoroughly learns what each customer needs, brainstorms possible solutions, and offers the solution that works best for its customer. The final decision about what to do is always made by the customer.

The teams in a customized enterprise are composed of diverse people who can easily work with others. Each team learns about its customer's industry, competition, and unique challenges. They partner with the customer, brainstorm, experiment, and recommend solutions. This enterprise typically builds long-term relationships with its customers. Leaders in this enterprise are participative. Their primary focus is on team building, consensus decision-making, and helping the team and the team's customer come to the best decision possible.

Public Relations companies like Ogilvy & Mather or Edelman are customized enterprises. Other examples of this kind of enterprise are executive search firms, realty companies and custom marketing firms.

IN THIS CHAPTER, YOU WILL LEARN:

- How exactly customers need to be approached in this kind of enterprise

- The right culture for a customized enterprise
- How fifteen culture drivers (decision-making, hiring, performance management, compensation, and eleven more) need to be practiced
- The right leadership approach for a customized enterprise
- How three leadership drivers need to be practiced

The Customized Enterprise Customer Promise and How It Must Approach Its Customers

ABT Interiors specializes in the design and implementation of custom commercial interiors. Its customers are restaurants, schools and universities, bars, and retail shops, to name a few. The company grew steadily for quite a few years but then ran into trouble. Growth had stalled, customers were complaining, leaders were at odds with one another, and people were refusing to cooperate with one another. Our analytics revealed that leaders and employees believed their customer promise to be *best-in-class.*

This was a very telling result. ABT was promising a customized solution—an interior that was tailored specifically for each customer, but the majority of ABT leaders and employees believed that the company's customer promise was best-in-class. These two kinds of enterprises are complete opposites of one another. People were not conscious of this major disconnect because they didn't know that such a distinction existed in the first place. With all the best intentions, ABT leaders and employees were unknowingly in a major tug of war with one another, and this clash of mind-sets was the root cause of their problems.

The customer promise of a customized enterprise is premised on the notion that its customers are paying for a close, highly attentive, synergistic relationship and effective customization of a product or service. Its value proposition is that it will provide a solution for its customer that is tailored exactly to what the customer needs. The customer can be an individual person, a company, a department within a company, or a class of people, such as a sub-community within a city. The central focus is *unique customer goal attainment.*

The customized solution for customers means that each unique customer receives a different solution. The solution is tailored for each singular customer. The best-in-class solution is created from within and then offered to any and every customer who wants to pay for it. Best-in-class customers all receive the same product or service; customized customers each receive something different.

The problems that ABT Interiors was experiencing are *symptoms* of significant *hidden disconnections* that are the root cause of those symptoms. Wrestling with the symptoms will not cause the real problem(s) to go away and, indeed, will cause more symptoms to appear. Once ABT's leaders and employees understood these distinctions and what they meant in practice, they had a clear pathway for renewing the company. This set the stage for how to go forward.

As soon as ABT's leaders learned about the four fundamentally different customer promises, they quickly agreed that the company's customer promise was customized. When our analytics showed that they and their employees believed that the company had a best-in-class customer promise, it was clear to them what was underneath the problems that they were having. Their customers were expecting to get a solution tailored just for them, but they were continually offered what was universally best (and the most expensive). Salespeople were showing prospects a catalog of interiors and trying to convince prospects to buy those with the highest price(s) instead of letting the teams who knew the customers work with those customers to come up with the best interior for them, at a price that they could afford. Even when teams had met with their unique customer to thoroughly understand what the customer specifically needed, the salespeople would undo their efforts by pushing the highest-priced product. One part of the company was canceling out what another part was doing. On one occasion, the customer told the design team that it could afford only a particular brand of tables and chairs for the school's cafeteria on a Monday. On Tuesday, two ABT salespeople showed up at that same customer's company, met with the two executives who had attended the meeting the day before, and tried to convince them that they needed to purchase a premium (and very expensive) brand of tables and chairs. The two salespeople did not even know that the meeting the day before had occurred. Right hands were undoing what left hands were doing and vice versa.

ABT's leaders met with the rest of the company, explained the difference between customized and best-in-class enterprises, declared customized as the company's customer promise, and described the changes that needed to be made. By far the biggest change occurred in sales and marketing. Marketing changed to exclusively focus on satisfied customers and what their customized interiors looked like. Salespeople changed to focus exclusively on generating leads and filling the company's pipeline. Designers created diverse teams for each customer and, in effect, these teams "made the sale" for ABT. These changes alone significantly increased satisfied customers and revenues (over time).

This enterprise works to understand its customer in depth. Ideally, it builds a long-term, lasting relationship with each customer. It is in a battle for scope with its competitors. It grows with each customer over the long haul. It thinks total solution. It keeps asking, "What else can we offer that would benefit our customer?"

For example, after completing the interior for a new restaurant, two ABT engineers came up with the idea that ABT could design and install a dining area for that same customer that was outside and in front of the interior restaurant. The customer liked that idea and went ahead with the recommendation. Dedicating an individual or team to each customer and doing as much as possible to keep this connection between people continuous is important because doing so helps the provider gain a much fuller understanding of what each customer needs, over a longer time frame.

Residential real estate is a customized enterprise. Real estate agent Patti Sorensen and one of her realtor colleagues were having lunch together one day, and Patti said, "I have a recently married couple who are looking for their first home. I know this couple well. I have been friends with them for ten years—long before they got married. We have looked at twenty-five homes and they can't agree on the kind of home that they want. Each one of them is very strong willed. I think we are spinning our wheels and going around in circles. I'm at a loss about what to do. Any ideas that about how I can handle this?" Her colleague asked, "Did the three of you start looking at houses right away?" When Patti said "yes," her colleague responded, "Why don't you ask each one of them to, independently, picture and describe the kind of house that each likes the best. Then, meet with them and ask them to take both preferred houses and see if they can put the two together—with your help. If they can do that (or come close to doing that), then the three of you could look for something on the market that matches their 'combined' house." Patti liked this idea and gave it a try. It took a quite a while to do it this way, but, three months later, they did find a house that they both liked and bought it. This is representative of what delivering on a customized promise to your customer looks like. People in this kind of enterprise have to be very adept at adapting to their customers, gaining an in-depth understanding of each of them, and, then, coming up with a way that is effective *for them.* You can't be in a hurry (unless your customer wants that), and you have to work within *their* parameters, not yours. You also need to team up with one or more of your colleagues because they can give you workable ideas that you didn't consider.

Residential realtors pretty much have to be ready for anything. Every customer is different. Each customer has specific and unique needs. They are quite unpredictable. This enterprise partners and bonds with its customers. All key decisions are made with the customer in the room. It co-develops a solution with its customers. The relationship is incremental, step-by-step. It moves in concert with its customer and continuously adapts to its customer. It goes with the customer's flow. When circumstances change for the customer, it changes along with the customer. If the customer needs to suspend working together for a while, then work suspends until the customer is ready to re-engage. Being flexible and adaptable is quite important.

Pricing, planning, sales, and budgeting in this enterprise are practiced in the following ways. Pricing is often very different with each customer. Prices and offerings reflect what each customer can afford. The structure of the relationship is all over the map. One customer wants to work on a retainer with you, another wants a quick project, another wants a trial run before making a decision to hire you, another wants you to work one way with a part of the company and a different way with another part. When customers simply don't have enough money, the provider who comes up with a less expensive, but close enough, alternative will be given the work.

Planning in this enterprise has to be process-driven. Plans need to be developed and revised all along the way, every fiscal year. Growth comes incrementally and unpredictably. Setting financial goals first is putting the cart before the horse. Part of *tracking* progress can and should be financial, but telling employees that, on the front end, they must primarily focus on revenue, cost control, and profit goals undermines what it takes for this kind of enterprise to succeed.

In a customized enterprise, the providers of the service and/or product are the salespeople for it. The sales cycle is long. It is crucial to keep viable prospects in the pipeline because continued work is by definition unpredictable. Customized enterprises will inevitably encounter periods of time when they have no work—especially when they are starting out. Establishing a separate sales department and asking these salespeople to close and increase sales with customers does not work. Selling this way in this kind of enterprise contradicts the enterprise's customer promise and is guaranteed to *reduce* sales. Once work begins with the customer, frequent "upselling" also backfires. If the customer wants more work done, the customer does the upselling itself by asking for more work.

A very large human resources consulting firm that primarily provided packaged services and products decided that it wanted to add an executive coaching service to its repertoire of offerings. The firm had a sales department that handled all sales for the company—across all of its services. The more the salespeople sold, the more money they made. The start-up coaching group was told to rely on the larger firm's sales department for getting customers. Well, the sales didn't happen. The salespeople kept trying to get the new coaching group to come up with pre-packaged services and products that made their sales job easier and quicker.

The salespeople never really understood what the coaching group was selling. They were incentivized to sell packages and products, but the coaching group was offering a process. The salespeople were after *volume*; the coaching group was after a long-term, steadily progressing, relationship. In addition, potential customers needed to get to know their coaches before buying. Senior executives and salespeople were operating from a predictable and dependable mind-set that was causing them to work at cross-purposes with the customized promise of the coaching group.

Budgeting works the same way as sales in customized enterprises. Typical budgeting processes do not work in this enterprise. If leaders in this enterprise call for a typical annual budgeting effort—where people are asked to commit to a certain revenue, cost, and profit figure for the whole fiscal year—they will predictably be very frustrated every year. Customer acquisition in this kind of enterprise cannot be predicted. A small customized enterprise could acquire a new client, say in the month of March, and that client could end up accounting for 50 percent of the year's total revenue.

The human resources firm described a few paragraphs earlier had senior executives who kept insisting that the coaching group provide them with a quarterly and annual budget. The team running the coaching group had no idea what was going to happen—revenue-wise. Costs are more easily budgeted, but if a large unanticipated customer comes in the door, costs can quickly get out of budget. The customized enterprise needs to develop a "running budget" that keeps everyone up-to-speed about revenues, costs, and profits on a continuing basis.

Linking incentive pay to such a budget doesn't work. This is an enterprise in flow. If you try to predict revenue and profit at the beginning of your fiscal year and tie financial incentives to budget adherence, you will inevitably end up needlessly (and annoyingly) muscling your customers. This will *reduce* your revenue and profit because it contradicts your promise in the eyes of your customers. The key is to keep the pipeline full. The cost of customer acquisition is typically high.

Working with customers often takes the shape of action research— trial tests, small experiments at first, testing the waters, developing prototypes. IDEO's "design process" is exactly this. Once ABT understood the customized promise and its required culture and leadership, it built prototypes, met with customers, and made sure that ABT was on the right track. The company went step-by-step with each customer and adapted to the customer's voiced needs and time frame. If the customer wanted ten trial runs, the customer received ten trial runs. The delivery process was incremental. ABT would take a step and then get back to the customer to get feedback.

People in this enterprise know they are approaching their customers effectively when customers tell them that their product or service benefited them and when they call and tell them they want more work. It is a very difficult business to scale. Growth comes slowly.

When a customized enterprise is publicly traded, life can get quite complicated. Everything investors expect—consistent growth, year-over-year improvement, reliable earnings estimates, etc., contradicts how business happens in a customized enterprise. The solution for this issue is beyond the scope of this book, but it is worth highlighting when it comes to describing how this enterprise works with its customers and generates revenue.

Custom home builders (like Schumacher Homes), custom marketing consulting firms (like Core 3 Solutions), and public relations firms (like Burson-Marsteller and Edelman) are all examples of customized enterprises. Edelman describes itself as a "marketing firm that partners with many of the world's largest and emerging businesses and organizations, helping them evolve, promote and protect their brands and reputations." WE, the world's second largest PR firm, "partners with clients to transform their business through storytelling, in many different forms." Executive search firms like Spencer Stuart and custom interior design companies are customized enterprises.

Here's an example of how *not* to work with a customer if you are a customized enterprise. This actually happened with one of our clients—no names are used in order to protect anonymity.

I assisted a midsize university in the selection of a new marketing vice president. The school hired an executive search firm that specialized in finding candidates for university marketing departments. The firm stated that it "can complete a search in four to five weeks." An executive search firm, by its very nature, is a customized enterprise.

The two search firm consultants spent a day touring the city where the university was located and the university's campus. They also spent two hours asking the search committee to spell out the qualifications needed for the position. The majority of contact with the firm had to be initiated by the search committee members because they were not hearing much from the firm. The firm presented its candidates in four weeks, but none of the candidates met the qualifications required—which technically delivered on the firm's promise to "complete a search in four to five weeks." Once it had presented the candidates, the firm devoted most of its time trying to sell the candidates to the committee and gave every impression that the *candidates* were the firm's true customers. The firm's representative spent all of her time touting the specific characteristics of each individual. These characteristics did fit *some* of the qualifications but brushed off and/or minimized others. The search firm had initially claimed that it was a better choice than its competition because it could determine "fit with your culture" and the competition did not do that. Yet, when presenting candidates for the position, the firm never brought up "fit with culture" with the committee.

Four months later the university hired a person who had been recommended by a member of the board, not the search firm. Needless to say, the search committee was not satisfied with the service provided by the search firm or its $30,000 fee.

The Right Culture for a Customized Enterprise and How Fifteen Cultural Drivers Must Be Practiced

Because ABT must be a customized enterprise, the right culture for ABT is a collaboration culture. When we measured ABT's core culture and culture drivers, we found:

- Core culture is *control*
- Summary of the fifteen culture drivers is:
  - Nature and use of power, decision-making, managing conflict, compensation, organizational structure, and role of employee is control
  - Teaming and people development is collaboration
  - Managing innovation and managing change is competence
  - Hiring is cultivation
  - Promotion, managing performance, information technology, and nature of work are unclear

ABT's predominant or central culture was control, which is a fit with a predictable and dependable enterprise, not a customized enterprise. A control culture operates to accomplish certainty, predictability, safety, or security. It has to stay in control or it will fail. It is centered on operations. But what a customized enterprise needs is a collaboration culture, which is all about combined effort, close connection with the customer, and bonding with the customer. It runs on teams and team structures. The search firm discussed above did not partner with or truly collaborate with the university's leaders. Instead, it tried to see what it could get away with. The firm just wanted to make a quick sale and move on.

Cultivation of the customer keeps the enrichment enterprise's values front and center. The realization of values is what drives this culture. Competence is all about distinction. The expertise of a best-in-class enterprise drives this culture. Ideas for what to sell come up from within the enterprise, from the culture's experts.

The collaboration culture essentially operates by building people into a team and empowering them to fully utilize one another as resources in order to provide each unique customer with a tailored solution. Customers are always a part of the teams in this enterprise and, as much as possible, the teams stay intact in order to provide continuity with each customer.

As the reader may recall from Chapter 1, the customized enterprise is an actuality-personal enterprise. It attends to immediate customer demand and is rooted in concrete and tangible reality. It focuses on getting today's job done for its customers, doing and producing now. It makes decisions by relying on a single person or a team's consensual *judgment*. This combination of actuality attentional focus and personal decision-making is a powerful shaper of the customized enterprise's culture. It pulls this culture into an inevitable set of behaviors.

Coldwell Banker is a realty business. Residential realty businesses are prototypical customized enterprises. If you put yourself in the shoes of a Coldwell Banker residential real estate agent, your work life goes something like this. You have five different customers who are looking for a house to buy. Each customer wants something different, goes by their own unique time clock, has different tastes, has a particular amount of money they are willing to spend, wants to live in different neighborhoods, does or does not have children. And, this is just a beginning list. You have to adapt to each client, understand as much as possible what each is looking for, be patient with one customer, wait for one to call you because they do not like being disturbed, answer another's call every day, etc.

You have to pay attention to each customer *now*. And, you have to be a co-judgment-maker with each one. There is no data-based way to make a decision. Including quantitative data (comparable prices, days on market, etc.) as part of the decision-making process is typical, but primary decision-making is collegial and collective judgment based. It is based on experimentation, trial and error, and testing in the real world.

When it comes to culture and leadership, there is a very important distinction to keep in mind. Culture's fifteen drivers are *practiced* differently in each of the four enterprises. This is also true for the three leadership drivers. The principles of each apply to all four enterprises, but each of the four enterprises practices them differently.

For example, the principle of teaming applies to all four enterprises, but teaming is practiced differently in each. Teaming is at the center of the collaboration culture. The customer is an integral part of the team and the final decision-maker. The team tries to reach consensus as much as possible. Teaming in a predictable and dependable culture is cross-functional in nature. Function A teams with functions B and C to solve an operational problem and then disbands. Decisions are based on facts and data. In a competence culture, teaming is win-lose. Being right is what's important. Expertise, facts, and data are the basis of decision-making. Teams are composed of the right experts needed to achieve a certain objective—which could take a week or five years. In a cultivation culture, teaming is based on what it takes to realize strongly held values. Teams typically stay together for long periods of time. Team composition varies all over the board in this culture.

The culture driver results depicted above became the elements of a change roadmap for ABT. The company implemented a systematic effort to make company practices consistent with a collaboration culture. Design, estimating, engineering, quality control, and manufacturing were determined to be ABT's "core" culture—the work processes that drive delivery of ABT's customer promise. Representatives from each of these core work processes and each customer now constituted new customer-focused teams. These teams were trained in consensus decision-making and team management. Marketing, sales, accounting, information technology, and purchasing were identified as support cultures that needed to function in service to the core. Customer teams were given the power to decide because they were the only people in the company who had the information needed to do so. Compensation was changed to reward core teams and support units on customer satisfaction, revenue generation, and overall company profitability. All of this streamlined functions and relationships between units. Responsibilities were clarified.

In a customized enterprise decision-making is collegial, consensus oriented, organic, and very open to change. Decisions are made by teams, each of which is dedicated to a unique customer. Brainstorming is quite prevalent. Customers are closely involved in decision-making, all along the way. The customer always has the final "say" if consensus cannot be reached.

Managing change in a customized enterprise is essentially a matter of getting a team together, determining what is working and not working, and then coming up with the next initiative. Change is constant in this culture. It moves incrementally, step-by-step. It typically relies on "action research"—an action is taken, people see what happened, and then take the next step.

Managing performance is based on what works for the customer. People on the team manage the performance of others on the team. The team co-manages performance, if you will. It is basically a matter of determining what is working and not working and deciding what to do next. Innovation is managed the same way. New ideas and new methods should always be welcome. Then, innovations spring from trying to fit the needs of the customer—which vary from one customer to another.

ABT's leaders met on a regular basis with each customer and asked the customers how well they were being treated, what was working or not working, and whether or not they were satisfied with the results they were getting.

Conflict in a customized enterprise is necessary for success. Disagreements are needed just as much as agreements. At ABT, if manufacturing was unable to produce what the customer wanted, the customer and the team needed to know that. The same was true for estimating. If a customer had a ceiling for its costs and estimating determined that what was being considered would push the customer over that ceiling, everyone needed to know that. Diversity of judgments underpins success.

The nature of work in a customized enterprise is generalist oriented. Over time, people acquire a broad set of capabilities so that they can move in and out of various teams and provide a wide range of help for customers. People with a broad range of knowledge are needed.

The role of the employee is to collaborate, contribute, use others as resources, honor diversity, and commit to and identify with the character of the enterprise. People who rigidly adhere to a narrow specialty do not work out well in this culture.

This culture is typically structured in a group or cluster manner. Teaming is centered on a particular team of people dedicated to each unique customer. The customer is an equal and necessary team member. The team process is win-win.

Information technology is utilized to help people stay in continual contact with one another and with a team's customer. For example, ABT's information technology unit needed to provide support to the teams working with customers. IT designed software specifically to help each team stay closely connected with its particular customers. These teams decided whether or not they were getting what they needed. IT did not make the decision. IT *did* decide on *how* to design the software.

Employees are selected by how well they fit with the community and the team. Recruitment emphasizes versatility, energy, and ability and willingness to collaborate and build relationships. Selection is made by the team.

People development is highly experiential. On-the-job training is continual. It is "try and see what happens" oriented. Training and development is real-time, team based, and action oriented. It is issue focused—case studies are quite prevalent. Diversity in learning is fostered.

Promotion is based on the extent to which customers are served, development as a generalist, and ability and willingness to work well with others. Promotion is given to those who are willing to move around the organization, learn new skills, and channel their talents into what works for the whole enterprise.

This culture lives and dies on trust and goodwill. It is highly action oriented, spontaneous, and centered on doing whatever it takes to deliver on the enterprise's promise. Tolerance for ambiguity and frustration is important because so much ongoing adaptation with each customer is needed.

Central values in this culture are: trust, synergy, egalitarianism, diversity, community, spontaneity, affiliation, and optimism.

The Right Leadership for a Customized Enterprise and How Three Leadership Drivers Must Be Practiced

The right leadership for a customized enterprise is participative. When we measured ABT's leadership approach, we found the following:

- Core leadership is *directive*
- Building organizational capability is directive
- Setting direction and mobilizing commitment are unclear

ABT's predominant or central leadership was directive, which is a fit with a predictable and dependable enterprise, not a customized enterprise. Its leaders were making decisions based on their titles and how high they were in the hierarchy. They were primarily focused on company financials, revenues, costs, and profitability. Sales and marketing were trying to get customers to buy best-in-class interiors; designers and manufacturing were trying to make sure that what was being sold would actually work. All of these different mind-sets were confusing and alienating customers who kept getting mixed messages from the company. Where each leader was in the hierarchy really had nothing to do with effectively delivering on the company's customer promise. As you might imagine, this disconnected practice alone was a major contributor to ABT's slowdown in the marketplace.

The participative leader builds people into a team and empowers them to fully utilize one another as resources in order to provide each unique customer with a solution. Customers are always a part of the teams in this enterprise, and, as much as possible, the teams stay intact in order to provide continuity with each customer. A participative leader creates conditions whereby people can work effectively in teams and collaborate with the enterprise's customers. For example, ABT's team leaders regularly ask team members to talk about how well the process is working because human nature is to get caught up with ideas and neglect the process. The leader's essential job is one of *people process*. He or she designs teams, helps people on the team work together, builds trust within the team, and guides consensus decision-making. This leader fosters full and active participation by all and ongoing customer involvement in the team's judgment-making. He or she is a first among equals. Unlike in a predictable and dependable enterprise, the leader does not decide for others. He or she guides the process in order to enable the team to come to its own, collective, best judgment.

This leader fosters brainstorming and give-and-take. Each unique customer will be best served if the team assigned to that customer continually centers its best collective thinking on what works for each customer. For example, the executive search team leader for the university discussed above missed half the meetings with the committee, and when she did show up she hardly said a word. If she had practiced the participative approach, she would have treated her team and the search committee as one team and focused on the entire team's process. She would have encouraged everyone to voice their opinion, looked for areas of agreement and disagreement, helped people work through the areas of disagreement, and tried to bring everyone as close to consensus as possible.

The participative leader prefers to take action and get data until the best decision is clear. Being flexible, adaptable, and open-minded to the ideas of others is important. This leader manages ambiguity and conflict well and believes that effective management of conflict is essential to the enterprise's success. Consistently emphasizing the practical side of issues, the participative leader is quite application oriented. He or she enjoys negotiating, bargaining, and active experimentation.

The results of our measurement of core leadership and leadership drivers also became elements of the change roadmap for ABT. The company implemented a systematic effort to change the required leadership behaviors to participative. The leadership team went through participative leadership training and coached one another on how to be more effective participative leaders. This training included practical examples of how to set direction, mobilize people's commitment, and build organizational capability in a customized enterprise. Because ABT leaders were taking a directive approach to leading the company, they were, in effect, trying to control the uncontrollable. A customized enterprise grows iteratively and incrementally. It grows in fits and starts.

One year, it has so many customers that the company can't keep up and the next year customers are very hard to find. The leaders' essential focus needed to be on helping the teams connect with each customer and work collaboratively to meet the unique needs of each customer.

Leaders in a customized enterprise set direction by staying close to each customer and each class of customer. They emphasize capitalizing on opportunities and helping to determine ways to customize for each customer. They make sure to get teams involved in setting direction and deciding which classes of customers to pursue.

They mobilize commitment by building and preserving trust among and within teams. They capitalize on the power of relationships and emphasize the importance of everyone's active participation. They clarify how customer satisfaction keeps everyone successful and continually communicate satisfied customer messages to their teams. They ensure that customers are brought in and get involved in what it takes to build commitment.

Participative leaders build organizational capability by designing and building teams, fostering collaboration and group problem-solving, and pushing for consensus. They ensure that the customer is closely involved in every key decision. ABT's senior leaders met with team leaders and worked with them to understand exactly what deciding by consensus means and how to utilize conflict (differences of judgment) to ensure that everyone's ideas were getting heard. Participative leaders facilitate team decision-making. They seek customer-focused solutions and ensure continual customer involvement and co-problem solving. They continually spur others to action.

As changes were made in the company's approach with customers and culture, it became clear that how ABT was structured was getting in the way. The company's hierarchy greatly confused things. Leaders with higher titles were making decisions regarding the company's approach with customers that contradicted what teams had consensually decided. Role (titular) power was clashing with relationship power. The team, with its unique customer on the team, came to a collective judgment about what was needed to deliver on ABT's promise to that customer (after much discussion) and, then, a vice president would come in and direct the team to do something different. As might be imagined, this did not sit well with the team and, more important, it alienated the customer. Most important, that VP had no way of knowing the right decision because he or she had not been part of the process every step of the way. Project coordinators who were responsible for installing the interiors did what the VP of manufacturing directed them to do, not what customer-focused teams were learning from each customer.

So, leaders dismantled ABT's hierarchy and took people's titles away.

All of this was holding ABT back and stalling the enterprise's growth. Simply learning that ABT's customer promise was a customized one and what a customized promise called for regarding culture formation and leadership approach was the fundamental solution. ABT set about reshaping its culture into one of collaboration and its leadership approach into a participative one and progressively turned the enterprise around.

In general, the customized enterprise type has many strengths. It is naturally at home with diversity (the more the better) and managing conflict. Communication is open, free, and direct. It is inherently effective at building, developing, and utilizing teams. It naturally builds a community. It is quite adaptive and versatile. People readily develop ownership within the enterprise and help one another out.

Its weaknesses are that it can easily get caught up in groupthink, where people feel pressured to go along to get along. People can hold back from holding one another accountable. It tends to breed cliques. It can take collective agreement too far and stifle individual thinking. It is prone toward resisting planning and thinking too short term. When dealing with complex issues it can get hamstrung and stuck in an impasse.

To prevail in a win-lose marketplace, this enterprise must take a win-win approach with its customers. Put another way, if you overemphasize beating your competition and give in to the temptation to start muscling your customers to do that, you will lose in both arenas. This is most evident when it comes to timing. To effectively deliver on your promise to your customers you have to go with your customer's clock. Some customers are in a hurry, some are in no hurry at all. Others are in a hurry one minute and in a slowdown the next. People in this enterprise must be adaptive and able to go with the flow. They have to be ready for anything.

Of the four enterprises discussed in this book, the fate of this enterprise is the most perilously in the hands of its customers. The customers of an enrichment enterprise are inclined to be more forgiving, those of a best-in-class enterprise more disappointed, and those of a predictable and dependable enterprise more stuck with no options. Customers of the customized enterprise are so closely intertwined with a provider, the provider can lose its business every step of the way toward accomplishing results. If customers of this enterprise are not sure what outcome they are after (this happens more than one would think), they can start to get fickle and too easily put off. One of the customer's leaders can have a bad day and get upset with the provider, and then start lobbying with the rest of the leadership team to stop working with the provider. Because the connection between the provider and the recipient is so relational based, interpersonal conflicts can derail the whole effort.

The essence of a customized enterprise is partnership, trust, and empathy. Partnering, gaining trust, and empathizing are easier said than done. They require a great deal of patience, attention to the needs of customers, tact, and relational skills. Obvious self-interest dooms success. In this world, you can eventually acquire more business with a customer by convincing your customer that it should *not* buy something from you because it is not in the customer's best interest. Things can quickly get messy. Things are less straightforward here. You have to be ready for anything. But, it is very rewarding and you often make friends for life.

6

THE SYSTEM-CENTRIC
MIND-SET

Start and Stay with Your Living System

➤ ➤ ➤

The airline industry is a tough place to make a buck: too many competitors, price-sensitive customers, high capital intensity, boom-or-bust cyclicality, powerful suppliers, and often intransigent unions. But, Herb Kelleher, the co-founder and chairman of Southwest Airlines, did it.

From its start in 1971, Southwest has grown into the fourth-largest airline in the United States, with thirty consecutive years of profitability, in an industry in which no other company has been profitable for even five straight years. Total shareholder returns during that period were almost double the returns of the S&P 500. Southwest has managed to accrue a market capitalization larger than the rest of America's airlines combined.

Southwest's achievements are widely attributed to its relentless focus—draw travelers not from other airlines but from buses, cars, and trains by providing them the least expensive and fastest service available. But, at the center of Southwest's success are its culture and employees. According to Mr. Kelleher, the "spirit" of his people is the "most powerful thing of all." From the beginning, Southwest employees have been the most highly compensated in the airline industry—combining wage rates, profit-sharing, the full 401(k) match, and stock options. Executives from other airlines have met with Kelleher to ask him what his secret is, and his answer to them is "treat your people well and they will treat you well." Kelleher says that they all go back home to their airlines "disappointed." They tell him that his answer is "too simple." Southwest's mission statement deals solely with people—customers, employees, and leaders. When Southwest executives have a question about customers, they go directly to customers and ask them. They do not dictate to or try to squeeze more and more money out of customers. They don't give customers less service for less; instead, they give more for less.

According to Kelleher, his competitors believe that the "business of business is business." Kelleher believes that the "business of business is people."

He's right. Your enterprise is a living people system. The three living elements of your enterprise are your customers, employees, and you and your fellow leaders. Your job as a leader is to set direction, unify these three, and create the systemic conditions for delivering on your promise to your customers. You, your fellow leaders, employees, and customers are an interdependent network—a living system, one of the four distinct types of enterprises described in the first five chapters of this book.

There is not one universal set of cultural and leadership practices that applies to every enterprise. There is not one universal way to approach all customers. The same principles (e.g., teaming and working together is good, managing performance is necessary, leaders need to set direction for their enterprises, effective decisions need to be made, etc.) apply to all four types of enterprises, but they are practiced differently in each one. Customers need to be approached and worked with differently in each.

Because there are four distinct living enterprises, you have to start with which one of the four is yours—customized, predictable and dependable, enrichment, or best-in-class—to know the appropriate ways to practice the cultural and leadership drivers described in the first five chapters of this book. You need to adopt a system-centric mind-set, not an individual-centric one. Individuals are important, but your individuals can only succeed and prosper within the kind of system required to deliver on your enterprise's customer promise. If you jump into leading and managing your individuals first, without knowing which kind of enterprise you are, you will unconsciously and unintentionally create contradictions and people problems and set your enterprise at cross-purposes with itself.

If you buy a book on steward leadership and try to apply its ideas to leading in a nuclear power plant, they won't work for you, despite the book's claim that this style of leadership applies to all enterprises. Steward leadership will work in a physical therapy treatment center. Incentivizing individual performance in a customized enterprise will backfire and create problems. It will work in a best-in-class enterprise.

Because of how highly we (and most Western economies) value individualism, most of us unconsciously and understandably operate from an individual-centric mind-set. We begin any change by developing individuals and aggregates of individuals—360-degree assessments, intra- and inter-personal traits and behaviors, private feedback meetings with individuals, wearable electronic monitoring of individuals, etc.

The real culture of profit and nonprofit enterprises has to do with creating conditions for you, your fellow leaders, and your people to fully deliver on your enterprise's customer promise. It should be driven by the nature of your business and what must actually be done in order for you to succeed in the marketplace. It is not some aggregation of individuals' beliefs, assumptions, or values.

Each of the four living people systems has to keep the network of its customers, employees, and leaders at the center of all endeavors and address these three living entities as a whole. Customers, employees, and leaders are interdependent. If you focus primarily on your individuals when managing their performance and don't connect individual performance to delivering on your customer promise, you will go off on a tangent and start spinning your wheels. The system has to come first— once it is set up properly, the way to practice performance management becomes clear and can be implemented.

This applies to all of the cultural and leadership drivers described in detail in Chapters 2–5. If you don't start with your kind of customer promise, culture, and leadership, then you are managing performance and making decisions in a vacuum. There is no commonly understood context for your judgment-making. So, your performance "review" invariably turns into intra-psychic or interpersonal analysis—personal attitudes, traits, behaviors, interactions with other people, etc. Effective performance management is tied to enterprise goal attainment and delivery on your enterprise's customer promise. Primarily focusing on individuals or an aggregate of individuals creates crosscurrents, roadblocks, and contradictions. It also misconstrues priorities.

This distinction between system-centric and individual-centric is not an either/or issue. It is both/and. Every enterprise is a system composed of individual people. Both the system and the individuals need to be attended to. A key message of this book is that leaders need to start at the system level because their enterprise type—the kind of customer promise they have—determines how the system and individuals need to be led and encultured.

IN THIS CHAPTER, YOU WILL LEARN:

- Why good management ideas so often fail
- The importance of viewing your enterprise as a living system
- That the will and energy to succeed are already present in your enterprise
- The big disconnector

Why Good Management Ideas Fail

Cartwright Space Systems (CSS) (pseudonym) is a multi-billion-dollar manufacturer of powerful, potentially harmful, and expensive rockets. These rockets must work the first time. There is no margin for error.

Senior executives hired a new VP of leadership and organizational development whose staff grew to ten. These people thought new leadership ideas would greatly enhance the skills of the company's leaders whose leadership approach and culture they found outmoded and ineffective. In their view, "command and control" was no longer a viable or effective way to lead and manage. Consensus decision-making and self-direction were, they thought, the way to go. So they initiated quality circles, participative leadership, self-directed teams, quality of work life and human potential development.

After eight years, all of these professionals had been asked to leave. CSS had spent millions on their ideas, but the only ones incorporated into the day-to-day workings of the company were "statistical process control" and "manufacturing-requirements planning systems." Despite the company's best efforts, the other ideas simply didn't work.

All of these leadership and organizational development professionals were good-willed, bright, and highly capable, but their ideas did not fit with a predictable and dependable enterprise. Except for statistical process control and manufacturing-requirements planning systems, they were all much more of a fit with either a customized or an enrichment enterprise. As one VP said, "We have to base our decisions on what the specifications and the data tell us, not on some team's consensus."

He was right. CSS designed and manufactured rockets that had to work the first time—people's lives were at stake. The company had to keep its operations in control. The participative, consensus-based, and human-potential-development leadership that the leadership and organizational development professionals were pushing for only got in the way.

That's because CSS, like every other enterprise, is a particular kind of living system. It will only accept a decision-making approach that fits its own nature and what it needs to deliver on its particular customer promise, just as humans can only accept the right blood for their blood type. Statistical process control and manufacturing-requirements planning systems fit with CSS, a predictable and dependable enterprise. They were the right blood type.

In the last sixty-odd years, people have come up with many good management ideas. Used in the right type of enterprise, some work and make a contribution. But what characterizes them all is that they are premised on an individual-centric mind-set and claim that "one size fits all." It does not. In fact, by claiming that they will work for all enterprises, these management ideas often do more harm than good. Figure 6-1, on page 98, shows which management ideas fit which living enterprise types.

This is not an exhaustive list. In and of themselves, each is a good management idea. It just needs to fit with the appropriate enterprise. If it doesn't fit, it won't work. If you bring "best practices" into a public relations firm, a customized enterprise, they won't work because the PR firm needs to offer what each unique customer needs and can afford. Injecting "best practices" only causes confusion and contradictions. If you try to implement values-based leadership in a nuclear power plant, it won't work. It not only won't work, it could do great harm. The West Point approach to management won't work in a day care center. Win-win decision-making won't work in a high-technology company.

A Corporate Executive Board (CEB) survey of C-suite executives (circa 2016) indicated that enterprises will require significantly higher performance from their executive-level direct reports in the future. Less than 20 percent of these C-suite leaders had confidence that their executives could stand the test.

Customized	Predictable and Dependable
■ Holocracy	■ Vertical De-integration
■ Teal Organization	■ Statistical Process Control (TQM)
■ Seeking Customer Loyalty	■ Business Process Reengineering
■ Self-Directed Teams	■ Lean Manufacturing ("Just in Time")
■ Open Offices	■ Automated Distribution-and-Sales Systems
■ Quality Circles	■ Activity-Based Costing
■ Sensitivity Training	■ Focused Factories
■ High-Performance Work Teams	■ Zero-Based Budgeting
■ Brainstorming	■ Balanced Scorecard
■ The Collaborative Workplace	■ West Point Way of Leadership
■ Group-Oriented Leadership	■ Requisite Organization
■ The Human Side of Enterprise	■ Hope Is Not a Method
■ The New Partnership	■ The Leadership Engine
■ Quaker Method of Management	■ Leadership Pipeline

Enrichment	Best-in-Class
■ Flexible Organizations	■ Knowledge-Capital Measures
■ Industrial Ecologies	■ Benchmarking
■ Seeking Employee Commitment	■ Best Practices
■ Human Potential Movement	■ Imitating the "Excellent" Companies
■ Quality of Work Life	■ Core Competencies
■ Spirit at Work	■ Constant Innovation
■ Leadership as an Art	■ Performance-Based Compensation
■ Principle-Centered Leadership	■ Managerial Grid
■ Enlightened Leadership	■ Matrix Management
■ Steward Leadership	■ High Output Management
■ Synchronicity	■ Meritocracy Leadership
■ Values-Based Leadership	■ Scrum/Agile Product Development
■ The Strategic Heart	
■ Leadership Challenge	
■ Humanistic Management	

Figure 6-1. Management Idea by Living Enterprise

Survey results indicated that a large part of the problem has to do with the high failure rate of outside executive hires. Outside hires take twice as long to ramp up as a leader promoted from within. C-suite executives report that only one out of five executives hired from outside are viewed as high performers at the end of their first year in house. And ultimately, of the 40 percent of leaders who are hired from outside each year, nearly half fail within the first eighteen months. After studying more than 320 leaders in thirty-six enterprises, CEB found that the primary reason for these failures was that these leaders from the outside didn't fit well with the people whom they inherited.

Given our individual-centric mind-set, we will be tempted to chalk this up to something like "lack of emotional intelligence," or "poor team player," or some other intrapersonal or interpersonal issue. While that may sometimes be true, more often than not something else is going on. The fact that almost 50 percent of all outside hires eventually fail suggests that such failures are symptoms of a deeper and hidden systemic problem, namely that those new leaders are disconnected from the kind of living people system that they joined as soon as they walked in the door. Ron Johnson left Apple, a best-in-class enterprise, to run J. C. Penney, a predictable and dependable enterprise. That outside hire backfired. Carly Fiorina, a best-in-class leader, was a disconnection with Hewlett Packard, a customized enterprise. That fell apart. This is not meant as a slap at Ron Johnson or Carly Fiorina or anyone else. Ron Johnson and Carly Fiorina simply believed that their leadership approach was the right one for their companies when it wasn't. The message here is that their approaches did not fit J. C. Penney's or HP's customer promises and cultures.

If a leader brings his or her leadership approach into an enterprise that requires a different approach, it disrupts that system and creates crosscurrents and contradictions. Symptoms start showing up, creating more crosscurrents, contradictions, and additional symptoms while the root cause of them all—the clashes between customer promise, culture, and leadership—stays hidden. The "people issues" listed in the Introduction are all symptoms. Most of the time, the root cause of all of them is that cultural drivers and/or leadership drivers don't fit with their customer promise or one another.

The Importance of Viewing Your Enterprise as a Living System

In the year 2000, America Online (AOL) merged with Time Warner in a deal valued at $165 billion. So far, it is the second largest merger in history. When the deal was announced, Steven Case, co-founder of AOL said, "This is a historic moment in which new media has truly come of age." CEO Gerald Levin of Time Warner said, "Because AOL takes us to the Internet, our merger with AOL will unleash immense possibilities for economic growth." Case and Levin knew that media and the Internet would soon be merging—so combining Time Warner and AOL would put the newly merged company way ahead of the competition. The announcement was hailed by many as a momentous coming of age for the Internet and the triumph of the New Economy.

Within a year, the two companies hated one another. They had completely different kinds of customers and customer promises. Employees from both companies continually clashed with one another, and leaders from each company spent their time blaming one another for the financial losses that soon began piling up. Thousands lost their jobs. There were countless executive upheavals. Ten years later, the combined values of the two companies, which are now separated, was one-seventh of their combined worth on the day of the merger. To this day, the Time Warner–AOL merger is taught in business schools as one of the worst transactions in history. What happened?

Executives from both companies attribute the failure of the merger to market circumstances (the dot-com bubble burst), the slowdown of advertising, and the change in how to access the Internet. While these issues were definitely a factor, the major reason was the clash of customer bases, cultures, and leadership approaches. These two companies were oil and water. Time Warner was a predictable and dependable enterprise and AOL was a best-in-class enterprise. They differed on almost everything: whose leadership approach was better, how to decide, who had what kind of power, structure, design of work, and much more.

Where they really differed was in their customer promises, which meant that their living systems (networks) were completely different. Each had developed its own way of connecting customers, employees, and leaders. Their financially motivated merger ignored the fact that they were fundamentally different living systems and thus almost killed both, reducing their combined financial values by 86 percent. Put starkly, by primarily viewing their two enterprises as financial vehicles (more revenues, cost cutting, and layoffs and more profits) and not as living systems, they almost completely destroyed them.

They are not alone. Estimates vary, but somewhere between 50 and 83 percent of all mergers and acquisitions fail. The cumulative financial and human cost is astronomical. This has been the case for many years, and little headway has been made in getting to the bottom of the problem.

Leaders need to learn a different way of thinking—adopt a living system–centric mind-set. They need to define a merger or acquisition as a combining of two distinct living people systems, each of which is composed of a highly interdependent network of customers, employees, and leaders. They need to remember that each is a whole in and of itself and neither is reducible to its parts.

In a merger or acquisition, how the new enterprise is led and what kind of culture it develops should be determined by the new enterprise's customer promise. Separately, each enterprise has developed its own leadership approach and culture and, for a merger to work, the two merged enterprises need to create a new living system. All too often, the leadership and culture of the new enterprise is determined by financial engineering, cost accounting, and revenue estimating. Finance, accounting, market analysis, historical revenue analysis, legal due diligence, etc. are important. But, they shouldn't determine the new enterprise's leadership and culture. The customer promise of the new enterprise should determine that. Because this is misunderstood, upwards of 83 percent of all mergers and acquisitions don't work.

Marcus Aurelius said, "If a thing is not good for the hive, it is not good for the bee." Each individual bee needs the hive, but the hive does not need every individual bee. The hive systematizes the bee. Peter Drucker, perhaps the greatest thinker about leadership and management, said, "There is one fundamental insight underlying all management science. It is that the business enterprise is a system of the highest order: a system whose parts are human beings contributing voluntarily . . . to a joint venture. And one thing characterizes all genuine systems . . . : it is interdependence."

Interdependence means that your customers, employees, you, and your fellow leaders are interdependent and form a unified whole, a whole greater than the sum of its parts. Every enterprise is a living people system with three living elements: customers, employees, and leaders. Customers are not "outside" of your enterprise; the customer-employee-leader system is your enterprise. The more closely connected they are, the more successful you will be.

Your central focus needs to be the quality and extent to which your leaders and employees are delivering on your enterprise's customer promise—the essence of what effective performance means. The Time Warner/AOL merger did not work because each company had developed its own distinct and unified whole and a powerful interdependency between its customers, employees, and leaders. Each had developed its own living network, its own "reality." And the leaders ignored those realities—the living system in each company.

Your enterprise is not a machine. It may have machinelike characteristics, but it is not a machine, though many try to make it one by commoditizing, mechanizing, engineering, technologizing, and monetizing their enterprise. The vice president of engineering at a high-tech social media company has invented an approach to leadership based on quantum mechanics. He believes that setting up a group of employees is equivalent to setting up a "machine" because doing so will "give you a ton of leverage." His belief is that the effective approach to leadership is to design a machine with "few dependencies, single owners and minimal decision points." Now, employees are required to wear electronic badges and monitors that track their movements, face-to-face encounters, speech patterns, vocal intonations, and even posture. Some claim that "today's workplace centers on digital technologies" and these technologies "keep employees engaged."

When Yahoo laid off 600 employees in 2016, Marissa Mayer, CEO, labeled the action a "remix." We label our customers "ratepayers," "consumers," "targets," and "users." Employees are "wage earners," "human capital." Quite a bit of work has been done to numerically establish the "ROI on individuals." One financial analyst recently wrote that when it comes to determining the "value of people," that determination is accomplished by a metric called "purchase price allocation (PPA)." This estimate of the value of people is not "booked on a financial statement." It is "recorded as goodwill."

Your enterprise is biological, not mechanical.

Will and Energy to Succeed Are Already Present

McMoran and Haney (pseudonym) is a midsize litigation law firm that was stuck. It was in its sixth year as a firm and, for some reason, it couldn't grow any further. Some of the firm's very capable attorneys were starting to get disgruntled, and a few had left to go to other firms. A couple of big customers had decided to go with other law firms, and John McMoran and Frank Haney, the firm's two partners, were unsure why. John said to Frank, "I'm at my wit's end. For the life of me, I can't figure out what is holding us back. Do you have any idea?" Frank didn't, but suggested that they ask his good friend, Christine Sommers, to come in and talk to the attorneys and customers "to see if she can come up with something that we can't see. She is a very good attorney and she has built a very successful law firm." John agreed to give Frank's idea a try. Christine interviewed the firm's attorneys and the two customers who had gone with other law firms and, then, met with John and Frank to discuss what she had learned.

She said, "Well, I can't say for sure what is going on, but I can tell you that things changed after the two of you told the other attorneys that the teams assigned to each client should come to consensus before recommending plans of action to their clients. In the view of your attorneys, this directive backfired. It added considerable billable time to their deliberations, and clients were balking at the increased cost. Also, it didn't improve the quality of team decision-making. It made things worse. Too many consensually arrived-at decisions turned out to be wrong."

Christine's observation turned out to be the key to what had been happening. Because the only change John and Frank had made was to move to consensus decision-making, they asked their attorneys to go back to the way they had been making decisions in the past. That way of deciding was to strictly rely on the law and facts of the case and, if one person on the team was consistently right, the team went with her or his approach to winning the case. This worked because litigation is a win-lose proposition, not win-win. The teams needed to be right about how to win, not fully agree before making a decision. This simple, but important, change worked and the firm began growing again. Unknowingly, the two managing partners moved the firm from impersonal decision-making (which is required in order for a law firm to deliver on its customer promise) to personal decision-making and, thereby, changed the nature and use of power in the firm.

When John and Frank, with all the best intentions, asked the firm's attorneys to implement consensus decision-making, they unknowingly injected a major disconnect into the firm. McMoran and Haney is a best-in-class enterprise; customers hire the firm because they believe that it is the best at winning cases.

Consensus decision-making fits a customized enterprise. The central power in a law firm is expertise. In a customized enterprise, the customer is the final decision-maker. In a best-in-class enterprise, expertise (in this case, the firm's knowledge of the law) is the final decision-maker. John and Frank had instilled a contradiction they couldn't see into their living enterprise, causing the firm to falter. Negative energy appeared and affected the firm's attorneys and customers. Because McMoran and Haney's customers, employees, and leaders are interdependent, this one change impacted all three. It did not occur in isolation.

Living enterprises are not vacuums or some sort of sterilized chambers. They are filled with human energy. This energy continually flows—positively, negatively, or some combination of the two. According to Albert Einstein: "Everything is energy and that's all there is to it. This is not philosophy. This is physics." In living systems, reality is a network of dynamic and properly ordered connections, and the word dynamic has to do with energy.

The more your enterprise approaches your customers and practices its cultural and leadership drivers the right way, the more positive the energy flow. The less it does this, the more negative the energy flow. Requiring attorneys to decide by consensus was a disconnect and, because it didn't work and customers were tired of the bigger bills, the attorneys were losing, not winning. That caused their energy to turn negative. The wind had been taken out of their sails. A vicious cycle emerged. They started complaining (privately) with one another, which brought about more negative energy. They felt stuck, which created even more negative energy because they could not see their way out of the problem.

One living system parallel (there are many) occurs in our neurological pathways. Our neurological systems are a network. Electrical flow between neurons can be positive (excitatory), propagating electrical potential flow along the neural path to create further excitation, or negative (inhibitory), reducing or stopping the electrical potential along a pathway. What happens with the energy flow of people in a network mirrors what happens in our neural pathways.

Once McMoran and Haney's decision-making approach became based on expertise (the right approach for a best-in-class enterprise), rather than consensus (the right approach for a customized enterprise), the attorneys were set free and took it themselves from there. They did not need to be forced to do anything. They didn't need to be "engaged," "gamified," monitored by wearable electronic devices, sensitized, provided with badges, re-engineered, or stack ranked. As soon as they could see the forward path, they spontaneously took it. Their human spirit took over. A virtuous cycle emerged. By discovering and implementing the proper decision-making approach for their firm, Frank and John empowered their employees. Change happened spontaneously and naturally.

It's human nature to want to progress, thrive, succeed, move forward, flourish, and have a better life. This is true for customers, employees, and leaders. They will all embrace change when their living enterprise empowers them to change and they can see that the change will benefit them. The key is to create the conditions for this to happen. It is not to, overtly or covertly, force people to change or to centrally control employees by the use of technology or anything else. It is not to gain a "ton of leverage" over your employees, turn your employees into a "machine," to "keep them engaged," to "remix" them, or to "establish [their] ROI."

When you create the right conditions for success, your living enterprise is set free. Kurt Lewin, who is widely believed to be the creator of social psychology, discovered that a living social system can be successful only when its people have a high degree of freedom. If a system is stuck, leaders and employees can "unfreeze" it by giving people more freedom and identifying the forces that are driving movement toward a goal and the forces that are hindering that movement. The right cultural and leadership practices for the enterprise type drive movement toward the goal, empower your people, and "unfreeze" your enterprise.

McMoran and Haney's law firm was "frozen." As soon as expertise (the right kind of decision-making for a best-in-class enterprise) became the basis for decision-making again, the conditions for success were put in place and people's degree of freedom significantly increased. Attorneys were freed up and took it from there.

Put another way, people are inherently motivated to prosper, to contribute, to succeed, and to win. If you as a leader create the conditions for that to happen, you don't need to force anything. Trying to fix symptoms will get you nowhere. Building and implementing the right living system for your particular enterprise type will free up your people and empower them to succeed.

Eric Schmidt, recent chairman of Google, was asked how the company created its unique culture of workplace innovation. He said, "I think the one way to understand Google is to understand that we built it to *systematize* [author's italics] innovation. If you have a way in which new stuff keeps happening, then the culture evolves with that. You don't say 'we're going to preserve our culture.' Instead you build an innovation culture that will take care of itself."

Randy Papadellis, CEO of Ocean Spray, spends most of each day talking with the company's 700 growers—who produce two-thirds of the world's cranberry harvest. "I often say my title should be chief alignment officer, because most of my job is to make sure the interests of the growers are aligned with those of our suppliers and customers," says Papadellis. The growers are also the owners of the company. Ocean Spray is a worker-owned cooperative, one of over 30,000 in the United States that collectively generate revenues of $650 billion. This business model has been widely used since the mid-19th century in Europe.

The energy to grow your enterprise and to prosper is already present. People just need the right kind of living people system to set them free to do it. When you stay locked in an individual-centric mind-set, you focus on unhappiness, lack of engagement, unaligned values, boring work, lack of fun, etc. This leads to happiness consultants, surveys, software that equates "culture" with "aligned individual values," technological monitoring, awarding of badges, dashboards, etc. This is simply tilting at windmills. The answer is to create the correct conditions for success, unleash people's positive energy, get people on a winning track, recognize and reward their progress, and celebrate success.

The four enterprises described in this book distribute power differently. What power means is different in each of the four. Change, innovation, and development happen differently. Energy flows differently. Decision-making is practiced differently. Freedom is practiced differently.

Because of our individual-centric mind-set, we fractionate our living system and, unknowingly, create contradictions and crosscurrents. I was in a meeting with the senior executives of a gas pipeline company when the VP of finance said, "Last year was the year of marketing. This year is the year of finance." What that means exactly is hard to fathom, but it does illustrate an unconscious way of thinking that is completely at odds with a system-centric approach. Apparently, the VP of finance believes that finance will take its turn at being at the center of the company for a year and, then, some other support function will get its turn. The center of a gas pipeline company is its pipelines! It is a predictable and dependable enterprise. Its center is pipeline operations. Finance needs to function in service to pipeline operations. Marketing needs to function in service to pipeline operations. You can outsource finance and marketing in a gas pipeline company; you cannot outsource pipeline operations.

If a pipeline company tries to make power emanate from finance or marketing, rather than pipeline operations, it creates destructive behaviors. Who is working for whom and priorities become unclear, conflict resolution gets confusing, and that causes people issues and other problems: wasted money and time, alienated customers, and reduced revenues.

Every nonprofit and profit enterprise exists to deliver on its promise to the customer. Once you are clear about which of the four living enterprises is yours, you can approach your customers and practice the right culture and leadership drivers for it.

The Big Disconnector

By the end of 1997, Microsoft was a hugely successful technology enterprise. Its software operating systems ran on 86.3 percent of all of the personal computers in the United States and its technology group was running on all cylinders. New ideas for delivering on the enterprise's customer promise were spontaneously emerging on a regular basis.

Then things began to change. The technology group was removed from a direct connection with Bill Gates, Microsoft's chairman, and began reporting to Steve Ballmer, CEO. Immediately the technology group was changed from one charged with dreaming up and producing new ideas to one required to report profits and losses right away. The leader of the technology group at Microsoft said, "We couldn't be focused any more on developing technology that was effective for consumers. Instead, all of a sudden, we had to look at this and say 'How are we going to use this to make money.' And, it was impossible." In every meeting, there were clear financial goals and outcomes, because everybody knew that the faster they could move the quicker the stock price would go up and the sooner they would be wealthy. Three years later, Microsoft had lost more than half its value.

Microsoft is a best-in-class enterprise. Its expertise makes it succeed. By forcing Microsoft's experts to function as quasi-accountants, Ballmer took his software engineers' eyes off the software development ball, brought about a serious disconnection, and set the stage for revenues to crater.

Martin Winterkorn was named the new CEO of Volkswagen (VW) in 2007. Winterkorn crafted a highly ambitious growth program, called

Strategy 2018, to make VW the world's top automaker and double its profits. Developing a new clean diesel engine, with better fuel economy than gasoline, and lower emissions, without a drop in performance, was how they were going to do it. Winterkorn ruled VW with an iron fist and put intense pressure on the engineers to meet these goals. The message from the top was: Meet these market share and profit goals or we will find someone else who can. However, the EPA implemented a new set of strict pollution limits for diesel engines and tougher gas-mileage rules. And there was no way that VW could meet Winterkorn's market share and profit goals unless the company made major gains in the United States.

The engineers were finding it impossible to come up with a technical fix to solve the problem, but they did come up with an idea that involved software. They developed software that, surreptitiously, would detect that a stationary emissions test was taking place and alert the engine-control system to adjust catalytic converters and exhaust systems to reduce pollutants. Doing this was illegal, but it was the only way that the engineers could keep Winterkorn happy. So they installed this software on the diesel engine cars. By making "double [the company's] profits" the goal, Winterkorn disconnected VW's senior leadership from the company's engineers. Winterkorn never asked his engineers if they had the expertise and capability to double VW's profits by 2018. He just demanded that they do it—and kept demanding it. The engineers were not able to accomplish what Winterkorn demanded, but Winterkorn and other senior executives didn't want to hear that and so the engineers cheated.

The United States discovered the ruse in 2015. In late June of 2016, the U.S. Justice Department announced that VW had agreed to pay $14.7 billion to resolve claims related to the diesel-emissions scandal. It is the largest class-action settlement ever. The agreement calls for VW to buy back as many as 470,000 automobiles. VW's worldwide reputation has been severely tarnished, which will inevitably lead to significant loss of future sales. Some estimate the long-term cost to VW at $48 billion. At the time of this writing (January 2017), there are indications that VW may go out of business completely. So far, six high-level managers have been indicted.

These two stories have to do with the individual-centric mind-set and power. The purpose of every enterprise is to deliver on its promise to its customer. If you promise quality dresses, then your job is to deliver quality dresses. If you promise a well-built house, then your job is to deliver a well-built house. If you promise safe, reliable, and dependable electricity, then you deliver that. If you are an executive search firm and you promise to find the right executive for your customer, then that is what you deliver. If you don't, you won't have satisfied customers—or any revenue, money, profits, market share, or stock that is worth anything. Eventually, you go out of business.

Profits are tomorrow's dollars. They allow you to stay in business and keep growing. When you make profits the goal, as Microsoft and VW did, you build in a major disconnection and that makes your enterprise lose money (hedge funds and investment firms are, presumably, an exception to this). If you make quick (e.g., perpetually increase profit, quarter by quarter) money accumulation the goal, you make this disconnection much worse. When you are a leader and you demand that everyone accumulate a lot of money for a certain set of individuals (including shareholders), you are really telling your employees and customers that these individuals are the *real customers*. You are also implicitly telling your employees and many of your fellow leaders and customers that they need to "get with the program" whether it is in their interest or not. It doesn't take much for people to interpret this as exploitation, trapping, or manipulation. You move out of the value creation business and into the (monetary) value extraction business. Going too far can get you into fraud or illegality (e.g., Enron, WorldCom, VW, and Tyco).

When you make money the goal, you are distorting the nature and use of *power* in your living people enterprise and creating a major disconnection. Each of the four living enterprises has its own central kind of power:

- Knowledgeable relationship (customized)
- Role/operations (predictable and dependable)
- Expertise (best-in-class)
- Belief (enrichment)

When you make profit the goal, you have created a fifth kind of power—money power. Now, what really counts (despite anything else that is said) is more and more money—quickly acquired. You have created a fifth kind of enterprise—a money mine that uses financial engineering (among other things) as a shovel. When you change the center of power to quick money accumulation, you build in huge contradictions and crosscurrents for many of your fellow leaders, your employees, and your customers. These crosscurrents significantly interfere with delivering on your customer promise, *and*, when that happens, you lose money (directly or by loss of opportunity dollars).

When you make profits the main goal, marketing and sales progressively switches from showing customers the benefits of their enterprise's offerings to manipulating customers. Finance moves to creating highly complex financial vehicles that allow the enterprise to extract as much money from customers as possible (often without customers knowing it). Power now means something very different than it meant before—now it means "get as much money from customers as you can, as quickly as you can." It basically puts your enterprise into some sort of directional limbo where the only choice people have is to tell you what you want to hear, fake their involvement, or cheat (as engineers at VW did) until they can find somewhere else to work.

Because there are only four fundamental customer promises, none of which is quick money accumulation, when money becomes the goal, employees feel lost and demoralized. Customers get tired of being manipulated and start looking at what the competition offers.

Eddie Lampert, CEO of Sears and, contiguously, CEO of his own hedge fund, ESL Investments, has taken Sears to the brink of bankruptcy. Sears has a very long history in American retail. Its Kenmore and Craftsman brands are iconic products that have graced the toolboxes and kitchens of American homes over the decades. Lampert's slow destruction of Sears shows what happens when you allow an enterprise to become driven by quick money accumulation rather than innovation and delivery of value to customers. Since Lampert took over, the value of the company has declined by 80 percent. From the day he became CEO, Lampert has used debt, stock buybacks, the sale of valuable real estate, and shuttering stores to extract millions for himself. He has now left a hollowed-out carcass of what was once a vibrant engine of our American economy.

This trend appears to have started about thirty years ago when Milton Friedman at the University of Chicago declared: "There is one and only one social responsibility of business—to *use* [this author's italics] its resources and engage in activities designed to increase its profits." Then, a few years later economists Michael Jensen and William Meckling proposed that the singular purpose of an enterprise is to "maximize shareholder value" and said that executives work exclusively for shareholders.

Together with new competition overseas, the pressure to respond to the short-term demands of Wall Street and shareholders has paved the way for an economy in which companies are increasingly disconnected from the state of the nation—selling key assets; cutting back on product support, customer assistance, research and development; laying off workers in huge waves; keeping average wages low; and threatening to move operations abroad in the face of regulations and taxes.

When continually increasing profits and maximizing shareholder value become the primary goal, all power becomes top-down—regardless of the type of enterprise. Continual financial enrichment of shareholders and their executive agents with large stock options drives the enterprise. Employees and customers are asked to adhere to the monetary demands coming from the "top"—current and eventual (those with stock options) shareholders, which distorts the use of power and ultimately disconnects the whole enterprise.

When you deliver on your customer promise, the enterprise's power is either knowledgeable relationship power (customized), role/operations power (predictable and dependable), belief power (enrichment), or expertise power (best-in-class). Profits are needed to keep your enterprise growing and succeeding, but they are not center stage. Putting them center stage does not work and, ironically, ultimately leads to financial decline. Jack Welch, former CEO of GE and a stalwart capitalist, told the *Financial Times* that "maximizing shareholder value is the dumbest idea in the world. Shareholder value maximization (SVM) has been an unmitigated failure and contributed to some very undesirable economic outcomes." In the 1970s the average lifespan of a company in the S&P 500 was twenty-seven years. In the latter half of the last decade, that lifespan had declined to fifteen years. In the era that ended in the mid-1970s somewhere between 10 and 20 percent of cash flow was regularly returned to shareholders. Under the rule of SVM, this has risen significantly, reaching 50 percent of cash flows just prior to 2008. By one estimate, since 1980, for every dollar in profits, 80 cents have gone to shareholders through dividends' share buybacks or other financial maneuvers. Far from providing capital to the corporate sector, shareholders have been extracting it from corporations.

As a result, the population of publicly held companies is shrinking rapidly. Companies are "going private" to escape the pressures of shareholder-primacy thinking. Between 1996 and 2015, the number of companies listed on U.S. exchanges declined from 7,322 to 3,700.

For many years, business writers have been talking about the purpose of every enterprise and warning about the peril of making profits the goal. Peter Drucker wrote: "To satisfy the customer is the mission and purpose of every business" and "No financial man will ever understand business because financial people think a company exists to make money. A company makes shoes, and no financial man understands that. They think money is real. Shoes are real. Money is an end result." Lou Gerstner, former CEO of IBM wrote: "In the end, an organization is nothing more than the collective capacity of its people to create value for the customer" and "the preoccupation with short-term earnings in the public-company environment . . . is quite destructive of longevity. This kind of short-term pressure on current earnings can lead to underinvestment in the long-term competitiveness of a business." After John Sculley was ousted from Apple and Steve Jobs had returned, Jobs said, "Sculley just wanted to focus on the money part and I wanted to focus on the quality of the products. My belief was that the money part follows the product quality part. Sculley's view was just the opposite." Walt Disney said: "I don't make movies to make money. I make money to make movies." George Merck, chairman and president of Merck & Company, Inc., said: "Medicine is for the patient, not for the profits."

To sum up, because your enterprise is a living people system composed of customers, employees, and leaders and these three kinds of people are interdependent, the success of your enterprise is rooted in the cultural and leadership practices between them. People issues and problems keep reappearing year after year because they are symptoms of using the wrong leadership and cultural practices for your customer promise. If these misfit practices and approaches are not addressed directly, the same problems will continue to resurface.

The purpose of every enterprise is to deliver on its promise to its customer. There are four universal customer promises and each one calls for distinct and properly ordered practices between customers, employees, and leaders. If practices from one kind of enterprise are implemented in one or more of the remaining three, they create contradictions, and people and systems work at cross-purposes. The wrong practices cause people issues and other problems. The solution is to think in a system-centric way and focus on what is going on among your customers, employees, and leaders. At its core, each enterprise is a living people system, not a machine. You cannot fix or repair it—you can only set things up so it can grow.

The human energy in living enterprises continually flows—positively, negatively, or some combination of the two. The more approach with customers and cultural and leadership practices are correctly linked together, the more positive the flow of energy. The less they are linked, the more negative the flow of energy. Linking them—creating the proper conditions for success—empowers people and sets them free to be their most energetic and productive. It is human nature to want to be happy, and for most people, that means using their talents as fully as they can, doing the best work they can, and building a better life for themselves.

The next five chapters provide you with a roadmap for creating these conditions, catalyzing positive energy, and delivering on your customer promise.

HOW TO CONNECT YOUR CUSTOMER PROMISE, CULTURE, AND LEADERSHIP

7

FOCUS

Establishing the Magnetic North for Your Enterprise

➤ ➤ ➤

Electrical engineering graduates Jerry Yang and David Filo started "Yet Another Hierarchical Officious Oracle" (Yahoo), a directory of other websites, in the middle of the dot-com frenzy. The two gambled that their small investment of time and money in Yahoo would pay off.

And at first, it did: By 1998, Yahoo was the most popular entry point for Web users. Yang and Filo quickly took the company public and in January 2000 (just two years later!), Yahoo's stock closed at an all-time high of $118.75 per share. Yang and Filo made numerous acquisitions. But, when the dot-com bubble burst in 2001, their stock price plunged to $8.11 per share and the company's roller-coaster ride began.

Yahoo went into the Internet search business and began competing with Google. It offered email storage. Executives along the way have called it a technology company, a media company, an advertising company, an entertainment company, and a digital magazine company. It has changed its mission statement twenty-five times since 1994.

In 2008, it had several large layoffs. In 2009, Carol Bartz replaced Yang as CEO but was replaced two years later by Tim Morse, Yahoo's CFO. In 2012, Scott Thompson was appointed the new CEO, and the company immediately announced more layoffs. Five months later, Thompson was replaced by Ross Levinsohn. Two months later, Levinsohn was replaced by Marissa Mayer.

But by June 2016, Mayer had laid off 15 percent of Yahoo's workforce. Several large shareholders are saying she should go. So far, Mayer has created five mission statements—when she took over, the company had twenty mission statements that had come and gone. As of this writing (fall 2016), by one estimate, Yahoo is worth -$8 billion (that's *minus* $8 billion).

What would you say Yahoo's customer promise is?

Yahoo was started to catch a big wave and it's been trying to do the same thing again and again for twenty-two years. It has never had a customer promise, because its leaders haven't really intended to build anything to last. Senior leaders and major shareholders (particularly hedge funds and venture capital funds) are the true customers and always have been. Yahoo has always been a kind of Internet casino where bettors place bets on various kinds of gambles. Yahoo executives would, very likely, deny this. However, if you look at their behavior, it is hard to draw any other conclusion. It is a risky place to invest in or work in.

Yahoo is one of the more obvious examples of an enterprise that has no focus. It has no observable customer promise. The premise of this book is that success hinges on establishing a core customer promise and then creating the conditions for people to deliver on that promise. This premise would predict that some *individuals* may succeed in hitting the monetary jackpot at Yahoo, but, in its current state, the enterprise itself will not last.

IN THIS CHAPTER, YOU WILL LEARN:

- What core and support customer promises mean
- How focus establishes your central goal
- How to tell if your enterprise is out of focus

What Core and Support Promises Mean

In 2013, Yahoo bought Tumblr for $1.1 billion. At the time, Tumblr, a microblogging website, had considerable promise but was losing money fast. Marissa Mayer, Yahoo's CEO, promised to "monetize" Tumblr and show Tumblr how to sell more advertising.

Tumblr is a customized enterprise. Customers go on Tumblr's site and customize their own messages (stories, photos, GIFs, links, quips, jokes,

MP3s, videos, fashion, art, and more). Yahoo, on the other hand, had no central or core customer promise.

Mayer left Tumblr alone for two years. But the company was stalled. She sat down with Tumblr's executive team and announced that she was merging Yahoo's sales team with Tumblr's sales team and putting both under a new executive who had little experience with Tumblr. He told his newly merged sales team that he had no idea what Tumblr did but thought it probably had something to do with the PDF business (which was not the case). At the same time, Mayer publicly announced that Tumblr was pushing to achieve a "$100 million sales goal" in one year. Tumblr's sales team was stunned. No one at Tumblr had been consulted about the new goal; Mayer seemed to have picked a number out of thin air. Pressure and frustration in sales bled into other departments.

Salespeople left in droves, and staff throughout the rest of Tumblr did too. Top Yahoo executives clashed with Tumblr and, mostly, just confused employees. One executive demanded that Tumblr make more sales one way and another executive demanded it make them a different way. Yahoo executives put more and more pressure on Tumblr to increase sales. Tumblr's sales did not increase—they plummeted. A year later, Mayer reversed course and separated the sales teams, and the two enterprises were back to each having its own sales team. But, by then, the damage had been done. Tumblr was losing market share and losing it fast. Two years later, it had never gotten close to the $100 million goal established by Mayer. Tumblr went from being one of the top 10 most downloaded free IOS apps to hovering around a rank of 100th. In January 2016, Mayer announced that the value of Tumblr had declined by $230 million. In July 2016, seven months later, it had declined by another $482 million.

Since Marissa Mayer took over as Yahoo's CEO she has made fifty-three acquisitions. When she merged sales teams, put a new executive in at the helm of Tumblr, and announced that Tumblr had to produce $100 million in sales in one year Tumblr was doomed. And, it turns out that Yahoo itself was doomed. At the end of July 2016 Yahoo was acquired by Verizon for $4.8 billion (though as of January 2017, hacks into Yahoo have some analysts wondering if the deal will actually go through). In 2002, Yahoo was worth $125 billion. That amounts to a 97 percent loss in value. Over the course of twenty-two years, some individuals cashed out, sold their Yahoo stock at the right time, and benefited monetarily. But Yahoo's lack of focus (clear customer promise) guaranteed that the enterprise itself would fail.

Yahoo's decisions doomed Tumblr because they drastically interrupted Tumblr's ability to deliver on the company's core customer promise. They pulled the company off center, confused employees, brought in a leader who had no idea what Tumblr's customer promise was, mixed up Yahoo and Tumblr sales teams, each of which had its own entrenched way of selling, and established a $100 million goal that changed Tumblr's *focus*. That goal was not based on what it would take to deliver on the company's customer promise. It is not clear what it was based on.

Revenue comes from living up to your customer promise; thus, how you generate revenue is different for each one of the four living enterprises. If your revenue comes from delivering a customized blogging website (that brings eyeballs to advertisers), then you generate revenue by increasing bloggers and informing existing and potential advertisers about how many people are utilizing your website, not by picking a revenue number out of thin air. Mayer was unconsciously demanding that the tail wag the dog. She exacerbated the problem by making the goal so high and by demanding that people meet it so quickly. Tumblr leaders and employees had to achieve an impossible goal on an impossible schedule while revenues were going down, not up. Mayer was setting up Tumblr to fail, right from the start. If you make money the focus, your enterprise loses money. Money is the result of fully and consistently delivering on your customer promise. The only exception to this is the Bureau of Engraving and Printing.

Mayer unconsciously injected competing agendas and competing priorities into the company. Instead of freeing up people to succeed, she created pushes and pulls that hamstrung them. She created *contradictions*. Tumblr began operating at cross-purposes with itself. She unintentionally slammed on the brakes, blocked Tumblr's energy, and stalled it out.

An enterprise has focus when its core customer promise is clear to, and fully understood by, everyone in the enterprise: customers, employees, leaders. Getting focus entails clarifying exactly what delivering on this promise looks like in behavior and what its implications are for every part of your enterprise. If this clarity does not exist, then people will naturally default to the behavior that is in their own self-interest, which inevitably leads to crosscurrents that hold you back. Study after study finds that when employees and leaders do not clearly understand their own enterprise's customer promise and what it will take to deliver on that promise, infighting for resources increases, responsibilities get confused, turf battles crop up, customers keep getting mixed messages, and their enterprises stall. A 2015 Gallup survey of almost 18 million customers found that only half of those customers believe that the companies that they do business with always deliver on what they promise. Gallup's research also reveals that only 27 percent of employees strongly agreed that they always deliver on the promises that they make to customers. Gallup's research results show that quite a number of enterprises lack a clear and fully understood customer promise.

A core customer promise is the enterprise's lead or primary customer promise. In many cases, every enterprise also has one or more *support* customer promises that are clear and fully understood. Tumblr's core customer promise is customized. Its support customer promise is predictable and dependable—the Tumblr website has to operate consistently, on demand, and reliably. The carefully designed use of support customer promises to enhance and distinguish the delivery of a core promise is an important way for an enterprise to gain and maintain distinct competitive advantage. The use of support customer promises can vary in type and intensity over the life cycle of an enterprise.

A retail bank is a predictable and dependable enterprise. U.S. Bank and Ally Bank have a predictable and dependable *core* customer promise. U.S. Bank operates 3,133 banking offices in twenty-five states. Ally Bank is strictly online and has no brick and mortar banking offices. U.S. Bank has a support customer promise of customized. When a customer goes into a branch to meet with a bank executive, that executive will try to provide services especially tailored to her. Ally Bank has a support customer promise of best-in-class. It utilizes its information technology expertise to provide all customers with quick, convenient banking services (e.g., checking accounts) that are better than anyone else's.

Support customer promises are utilized to give an enterprise a distinct competitive advantage of some kind. U.S. Bank and Ally Bank have the same core customer promise, but not the same support customer promises. A support customer promise can play a very strong role in one enterprise and a much weaker role in another.

You can't mix and match core customer promises or try to mush them together. You can establish a holding company of some sort (such as GE), but it is necessary to let the SBU's (strategic business units) function independently, thereby letting each focus on its own core customer promise. When Larry Page, CEO of Google, created a new holding company called Alphabet in 2015, he did so because it would give the kinds of businesses within Google their own specific focus. "Alphabet is a collection of companies. It allows us to run things independently that aren't very related. This new structure will allow us to keep tremendous *focus* [italics, this author] on the extraordinary opportunities we have inside of Google. This will make Google even better through greater focus," said Page. Page understands the importance of focus and how it centers and channels his people's work.

Your customer promise establishes what your customer expects to receive from you. It is a pledge. It is what you offer to your customer. It is the fundamental focus for action needed in order for you to provide significant added value to your customers—your value proposition. When you make a promise to your customer, you are asking your customer to put his or her trust in you to deliver on it. You are also establishing an interdependence with your customers—they are now *depending upon* you. Establishing your focus and ensuring that it is clear to everyone in your enterprise *properly orders your connection with your customer.*

Customer promise is the decider. It establishes your mind-set. It *centers* your thinking, energy, attention, and behavior and establishes your *core*. It sets your priorities, parameters, boundaries, and ground rules. It sets the stage for the *unification* of your enterprise—for all of the necessary connections between your customers, culture, and leadership. It is the bedrock of performance management. Individual and unit performance is essentially "managed" by tracking the extent to which your enterprise is living up to its customer promise. It is the central basis for decision-making. When conflict arises, the essential source of its resolution is answering what will advance or improve the delivery of your customer promise.

Yahoo's acquisition of Tumblr has not worked out for a number of reasons, but the main reason is that Yahoo has an unclear customer promise and Tumblr has a customized customer promise. If your organization has devoted great time and effort to deliver on one kind of customer promise and a second organization has done the same thing for a different kind of customer promise, you know from day one that you are going to have a hard time putting these two enterprises together. If these two enterprises are diametric opposites of one another, putting them together will be next to impossible. All of which is to say: Core customer promise must be front and center when any merger or acquisition is under consideration and you intend to put the two together. The probability is very high that your merger or acquisition will not work if the two enterprises have different customer promises.

Unless, and until, any management or leadership idea to improve your enterprise can be clearly linked to your customer promise it needs to be viewed with skepticism at the very least. If the clear link between the improvement idea and your customer promise cannot be made, the idea is very likely more tied to what the purveyor of the idea can do or to the personal value and belief system of the purveyor and nothing more. One size does not fit all. Statistical process control works in a nuclear power plant but not in a day care center. Consensus decision-making works in a public relations firm, but not in a high-technology company.

Why Focus Is Important

Scott Loftin, CNIC's (pseudonym) CEO, was a student of management theory and prided himself on being open to new management ideas and approaches. He was particularly intrigued by the ideas of partnering with customers, consensus decision-making, and self-directed teams. CNIC is a third-party administrator company. It provides claims administration for health insurance companies. Health insurance companies outsource claims administration to companies like CNIC to save money and to focus their own attention and energy on crafting and providing health insurance products.

CNIC'S CEO met with his leadership team and proposed that they lead the company in a much more participative way, implement consensus decision-making throughout the company, and assign teams, each of which partnered with a particular customer. His leadership team agreed with these ideas and quickly implemented them.

But, things did not go as planned. Customers started complaining that working with CNIC was confusing and too time-consuming; employees wanted more procedures and more detail about customer benefits and contracts; meetings were too long and often unnecessary; work processes needed more standardization; and supervisors were not given enough authority to make decisions. This all resulted in high employee turnover and increasingly dissatisfied customers. Revenues and profits had leveled off and were starting to show signs of decline.

When we administered our analytics, we found the following:

- Senior executives believed that CNIC's core customer promise was *customized*
- Supervisors and employees believed that CNIC's core customer promise was *predictable and dependable*

With the best of intentions, Scott and his leadership team unconsciously instituted changes within CNIC that fit with a customized customer promise. But, the nature of CNIC's business itself called for a predictable and dependable customer promise. CNIC's customers, insurance companies, expected accurate, dependable, efficient, quick, and less expensive claims administration. Claimants called into CNIC to gain clarity about what was in their insurance policies. CNIC employees had to follow what was in each policy. They didn't need to decide by consensus; they needed to explain what the policy required. In effect, CNIC's authority was the policy. Trying to come to consensus in a self-directed team only confused supervisors and employees and, actually, ran the risk of alienating its insurance company customers. The insurance companies had outsourced claims administration to CNIC because they wanted CNIC to do it better, more efficiently, and cheaper than they could. They didn't need a "partner," they needed a capable and easy-to-work-with implementer of a rather routine task. All of the problems that emerged were based in this disconnection.

Scott was quite well intentioned when he brought up his different management ideas; they just didn't properly line up with what it took to deliver on his company's core customer promise. In fact, they interfered with it. Once he and his leadership team understood this, they changed their approach with their customers, to decision-making, and their approach to teaming to what their core customer promise required. The problems went away and the company got back on track.

This is a common story. Because we unconsciously start from an individual-centric mind-set, we take it for granted that a CEO or senior executive (individually) can, like Scott, decide it would be better for the enterprise if he, the CEO, changed how decisions are made and customers approached. This book says: Operate from the system-centric mind-set first. Determine your core customer promise and then create the conditions required to deliver on it.

Focus is the magnetic north for your enterprise. It pinpoints your central *goal*. It identifies your destination, where you are going. If you don't know where you are going, any road will do. A clear focus ensures that everything flows from your customer promise. It shapes where your enterprise's power resides and how it flows. Your organization's culture and leadership are primarily formed and maintained by what must happen in order for you to succeed in your marketplace. Delivering on your core customer promise is your (living) *system* goal.

Which leads to another, very important, implication. If it's all about delivering on your customer promise, then the way to *manage* your living enterprise is to build and implement an enterprise-wide *customer goal attainment system*. This funnels everyone's attention and activity into delivery on the enterprise's customer promise. The system-centric approach of this book builds and manages an enterprise that has customer goal attainment at its nexus. Individual, unit, and group performance should be addressed in the context of goal attainment. Then, customer promise delivery goals can be set, plans and timelines built. Positive and negative feedback would then be treated as what is working and not working in that context. People would concentrate on helping one another accomplish the goal (including subgoals). The main emphasis of everyone's contribution would be on how well *we* are working together *as a system* to deliver on our promise to *our* customer. People would ask one another what can be done to attain goals—not wait for the company's artificial intelligence server to print out "every tiny detail of who proposed a key idea in a long-ago meeting and who managed the tasks to make it happen" (a performance management idea recently proposed by a technology consulting firm).

Progress would be continually monitored to learn what is working and not working. Success, problems, and failure then become simply feedback about what is working and not working regarding collective pursuit of the customer promise goal. People would focus on helping one another succeed (not worrying where they are ranked). Accomplishments would be celebrated all along the way. Leader, manager, and individual development would be primarily based on where people could improve on contributing to their customer goal attainment system.

Each of the four living enterprises described in this book has its own central kind of customer promise goal attainment. They are depicted in Figure 7-1.

Ideally, each enterprise would build a customer promise goal attainment system that fit its kind of living enterprise system. Support entities would operate in service to the parts of the enterprise that deliver directly on its customer promise—these are the support units' "customers."

Figure 7-1. Customer Promise Goal Attainment for Each Enterprise

Support units could have any one of the four customer promises—quasi-enterprises, if you will. Each support unit would build and implement its own customer goal attainment plan.

When this all gets built and implemented, your customer goal attainment system becomes the central template for managing your enterprise.

How to Tell If Your Enterprise Is Out of Focus

The Foundation for Promoting Democracy (FPD) (pseudonym) is a nongovernmental enterprise that supports sustainable democracy worldwide. It is an advocate for democracy as the political system of choice and has offices around the world. It collaborates with countries, regions, political parties, and nongovernmental organizations to help build democracy. It also engages in democracy research, writes research papers, and disseminates newsletters and position papers. Since 1995, it has added various offerings and grown very fast.

In 2005, it began having employee problems. Employees were increasingly dissatisfied and disengaged. Turnover was high and increasing. Employees complained about unclear priorities, duplication of work, and contradictory messages from leaders and managers.

These particular problems suggested an unclear "focus" as the root cause. When we administered our core customer promise assessment to leaders, managers, supervisors, and employees, the result was that people were split down the middle between customized and best-in-class.

This result led FPD's leaders to look at their offerings to their customers; what became clear was that, as the enterprise grew and added offerings, it was building in another customer promise alongside its initial customized promise. From the beginning, the enterprise had provided each customer with a tailored solution designed to help each unique customer move closer to operating as a democracy.

As time went on, however, the enterprise added a best-in-class promise—it conducted research, wrote position papers and newsletters, and built a comprehensive online library of democracy-building information for its customers to access and read. These two customer promises were mingled together in the enterprise's work with its customers. This entanglement was the root cause of FPD's employee problems. Customized and best-in-class are diametrically opposite living enterprises. Comingling them created day-in-and-day-out problems. In effect, these two opposite customer promises and what it took to deliver on them were canceling one another out. The solution was to separate the enterprise into two distinct enterprises (still under the umbrella of FPD) and let them function independently. Within six months, the problems went away.

All that FPD needed to do was practice leadership and cultural drivers in the appropriate way for its enterprise type. The organization could have tried interventions such as team building, communication workshops, leadership development, employee engagement development, technological electronic data gathering of what people said in various meetings or where they walked while in the building, or awarding employees different colored badges for "good" behavior, or exit interviews, or many other ideas. Yet all they had to do was learn about the four kinds of living enterprises and see that FPD was unconsciously trying to deliver two different customer promises (customized and best-in-class) comingled with one another and at the same time. It didn't help that these two promises were exact opposites of one another. The root cause was a system-centric disconnection, not an individual-centric undeveloped behavior of one kind or another (such as poor communication, low employee engagement, ineffective teaming, etc.).

A focus conflict is very likely the root cause when the following kinds of people problems show up: unclear priorities, duplication of work, mixed messages from leaders, confusion about where the enterprise is headed, customers wondering why one thing is said and something different happens, unclear or contradictory manner of working with customers, reluctance to getting feedback from customers, and a low level of accountability.

Linking culture and leadership to customer promise and realizing that customer promise determines what kind of culture and leadership is required takes your enterprise to the system-centric level and out of the individual-centric level. The system-centric mindset takes you to root causes; the individual-centric mindset takes you to symptoms. The success of your enterprise hinges on having a clear and fully understood core customer promise and properly ordering your culture and leadership practices to your unique promise. It all starts with your focus!

Starting with focus entails educating your fellow leaders, managers, supervisors, and employees about the four different customer promises and, then, asking those same people what they are actually experiencing. It is important to concentrate on what the enterprise is actually doing, not what people think should be happening. Once everyone sees and agrees on what is actually happening, they can talk about what should be happening. If the two are different, the solution is to focus on your customer promise and build a customer goal attainment system that delivers on that promise.

8

CONFIGURATION
Properly Connecting Core and Support Work Processes

➤ ➤ ➤

In 2002, GM used an ignition switch that failed to keep cars powered on, which led to moving stalls on highways. Drivers lost control of their cars, and the faulty switch prevented airbags from deploying. For the next eleven years, GM received notices from customers, dealers, the press, and its own employees about the faulty switches. Committee after committee at GM discussed the issue, but nothing was done.

For eleven years, no one took the responsibility to resolve the problem. For eleven years, legal, safety, quality control, manufacturing, engineering, the Product Recall Committee, the Product Investigations Group, Field Performance Assessment, and many other committees, including an Executive Action Decision Committee, discussed the moving stalls. Finally, in late 2013, the faulty ignition switch was deemed to be the problem and, six weeks later, the first vehicle recall was instituted.

To date (circa summer 2016), 124 deaths and 269 injuries have been attributed to the faulty ignition switch. GM has spent $2 billion just to resolve investigations, a security lawsuit, and injury claims. The company still faces sixteen (and counting) more lawsuits. It has recalled 12.59 million vehicles. It has paid an additional $900 million to settle a criminal probe with the Department of Justice, $300 million to shareholders, and $869 million to victims and their families.

The price of the ignition switch was 79 cents.

The GM ignition switch issue has many facets to it, all of which would take another book to cover. There are three parts to the story, however, that relate to this book:

- The astounding number of entities involved in solving this problem
- Silos
- The diffusion of responsibility

All of these—too many cooks in the kitchen, turf battles, and reluctance to be accountable—are symptoms of misconfiguration.

To understand configuration, think of it as an electrical power grid. The grid establishes where power resides (generation) and how it is distributed (flows). It is a properly interconnected network for delivering electricity from suppliers to consumers. It consists of generating stations that produce electrical power, high-voltage transmission lines that carry power to demand centers, and distribution lines that connect to individual customers. GM got its wires crossed. In a well-configured enterprise, power and energy flow efficiently to deliver on customer promise. Work processes that belong in the core are kept in the core and those that belong in support stay in support units; support units operate *in service to* the core.

This works differently in each one of the four enterprise types. GM is an auto design, manufacturing, and engineering enterprise—safety and quality control should be part of manufacturing and engineering. This is the core of GM. These work processes are central to GM's ability to deliver on its customer promise of predictable and dependable. There was no need for committees to get involved in the ignition switch problem. As soon as the core heard about it, those in the core should have gone vigorously after the *facts* and never given up until they had the facts and the solution in hand. But the company was misconfigured: manufacturing, engineering, safety, and quality control were seen and treated as independent entities and were not collectively reporting up to the same executive who should have had the final say. So eleven years went by and the cost to the company has been $4.069 billion so far. That's the cost of getting out of configuration, and many companies pay a high price for it—not as high in dollars as GM, but enough to cause a lot of damage or even put them out of business.

In this chapter, you will learn:

- Why configuration is important
- Signs of misconfiguration
- How to configure your enterprise

Why Configuration Is Important

Over the eleven-year span that GM addressed the ignition switch problem, there were something like twenty kinds of committees and more than fifty committee meetings. Some committees formed subcommittees consisting of representatives from a wide spectrum of functions across the company and numerous levels of employees, executives, managers, and supervisors. They just interfered with getting to the bottom of the problem and coming up with a solution. GM needed *facts*, not deliberations from ten different parts of the company. The configured approach would have determined the problem *within* the core and formed a project team composed of only the relevant resources there (in the core) to solve it. The charge to the project team would have been to find the problem and come up with a solution as fast as possible.

Herein lies the importance of configuration.

The big problem with GM's approach to determining the cause of the problem and its solution was that it drastically dispersed the nature and flow of *power* within the company. Many competing agendas were created. Who was responsible for what was unclear. Who had authority and who didn't was unclear. This resulted in lack of accountability. As deliberations went on and on, more injuries and deaths were occurring, which led to buck-passing, pushing everything "upstairs," and claims of ignorance. A destructive vicious cycle was created that compounded the problem (and the eventual costs).

Each of the four living enterprises has its own kind of power and its own kind of "grid." Power and authority are different in each of the four enterprises, but primary power always resides in the core of the enterprise—the work processes that directly deliver on the enterprise's promise. The center of power in a predictable and dependable enterprise is its operations, knowledgeable relationships in customized, expertise in best-in-class, and values in enrichment. In each of the four living enterprises, support's job is to help enable the core to succeed.

Configuration is important because it establishes the nature of power and the flow of that power within the core, within each support unit, and between the core and support units. It increases an enterprise's efficiency and timeliness. It prevents an enterprise from going off on tangents. It streamlines the conduct of work between different parts of the enterprise. It reduces conflict and frustration. It greatly improves goal attainment. Analogous to the electric grid, it enables the flow of positive energy and precludes the occurrence of negative energy.

During the ignition switch problem, the legal department at GM insisted that design, manufacturing, engineering, safety, and quality control be put on hold while the legal department edited all related documentation in order to avoid any possibility of lawsuits. For example, the department demanded that "problem" be replaced by "condition" or "matter," "safety" by "has potential safety implications," and "defect" by "does not perform to design." GM is not a legal enterprise. Legal needed to operate in service to the core of GM. The lawyers should have quickly met with the core and asked what the core needed from legal and how they could help. They also should have left the decision up to the core. The core did not need more obfuscation (it already had more than it needed); it needed facts to identify the root cause of the problem as quickly as possible. The good-willed intention of company leadership and legal notwithstanding, legal was delaying and complicating the resolution of the problem. The lawyers were just adding more crosscurrents to the whole resolution effort. By taking the reins and engaging in wordsmithing, they *increased* the probability that GM might run into legal problems. What needed to be documented was how hard and quickly the core was working in order to get to the bottom of the "problem."

The day that the ignition switch issue moved "out" from manufacturing and engineering was the day that the misconfiguration ball got rolling. The size alone of GM predicted that resolving the problem would take years. Misconfiguration always breeds more misconfiguration—more diffusion of responsibility and authority. Then more falls between the cracks and more critical information gets shelved and lost. Misconfiguration breeds frustration, and persistent frustration breeds fear, which breeds buck passing. A vicious cycle emerges.

As soon as GM leadership learned that a death or injury had occurred, they should have had the core get to the bottom of it right away, even if they found GM cars were not at fault. As soon as word got out, GM had a "problem," and the company needed to get to the bottom of it fast. But it could not, because it was misconfigured.

The core is the internal customer of the support units. Each support unit has its own customer promise, which may be the same as the enterprise's customer promise, but the support unit's customer promise, culture, and leadership need to operate in service to the core.

Signs of Misconfiguration

There is an impetus these days to create a new executive position called the chief customer officer (CCO). One proponent of this idea believes that someone has to be uniquely accountable for "driving the customer perspective throughout" the enterprise. This new executive is supposed to focus on acquiring new customers, keeping customers, providing customer service, and building customer relationships. He or she would spend time and energy figuring out who the enterprise's customers are and what they need and want. The person would "shape enterprise strategy where customers are concerned." Making this person a C-level executive "shows customers and employees just how important the customer is." One believer in this idea claims that the only company that does *not* need a CCO is Disney World because "the customer is so ingrained in their culture." Well, thank goodness for Disney World. At least one company is closely connected with its customers!

Seeing a need to put a CCO in place is a sure sign of misconfiguration— quite a few signs, in fact. If your enterprise needs a person with a C-level title to "drive" delivery on your customer promise, you have a lot of work ahead of you. Are your work processes focused on something else? If your employees are coming into work every day and they are not clear that they are there to deliver on your customer promise, what do they think they are there for? What are they actually doing? What are your CEO and other set of C-level executives focused on? If you need a CCO, your marketing, sales, and customer service units must be misconfigured. Establishing a separate executive and, presumably, a set of employees to demonstrate the importance of customers to customers (and employees) is tautological. It creates a major distortion that confuses both customers and employees. It is a disconnection and a contradiction. It actually *builds in* misconfiguration and belies reality.

If your enterprise needs someone with C-level titular power to "drive" (force) delivery on your customer promise, you need to work to get your whole enterprise reconfigured. It is a sign that your fellow leaders and employees are putting their time, attention, and energy into some number of unknown goals and objectives and that the different elements of your enterprise are misconfigured with one another.

There is another more subtle, but very damaging, misconfiguration going on here. Establishing a CCO assumes that every one of the four living enterprises needs an additional leader and set of work processes to "drive" delivery of its particular customer promise. Creating a CCO and giving him or her a set of work processes is giving this person a hierarchical (top-down) power that goes nowhere. To go back to the electrical power grid metaphor for a moment, creating a CCO is like creating an additional and unnecessary transmission line that is not connected to any other part of the grid and just duplicates what is already there. Whatever emerges from this new set of work processes will be useless and tangential. The CCO "function" will serve only to discredit the rest of your enterprise's leaders.

Any executive-level position created to "drive" a principle is a sign of misconfiguration. Positions such as chief (VP, director, manager, etc.) of "diversity," "sustainability," "engagement," "innovation," "creativity," "inspiration," "ethics," and "happiness" (yes, "chief happiness officer" does actually exist) will only create misconfiguration. The primary purview of leaders and employees is the extent to which their enterprise is living up to its customer promise! Creating a role, function, and set of work processes to day-in-and-day-out cause happiness will only create crosscurrents. All of these principles need to be addressed, in one way or another, by *all leaders* in the enterprise—as part of their responsibility as leaders.

Rigid silos are inherently creators of misconfiguration. Any entity in your enterprise that refuses to work interdependently is a problem. Silos are bottlenecks. Hoarding information or storing it so it can't be used interdependently creates misconfiguration. The common denominator here is what is or is not happening *between* support units and the core, between support units, and between work units *within* the core. The usual suspects are research and development and manufacturing, sales and marketing, engineering and sales, and hospital/clinic administration and patient care, to name a few.

Too many levels of management (anything over four) and/or too many direct reports (anything over seven) are signs of misconfiguration. When ASEA (Sweden) merged with the troubled Brown Boveri (Switzerland), Percy Barnevik, CEO, promptly sent a message to the thousands of managers at the company's headquarters in Zurich that everyone's job had to have "something to do with the customer." More than 3,000 bureaucrats were laid off or voluntarily left. Additionally, Barnevik created over 1,000 local offices. Decisions that had taken months now took a few days, at most. The new company took off and has been a huge success ever since.

When people are unclear about who is responsible for what across units, misconfiguration exists. For example, it is not uncommon for legal and human resources to struggle over EEO (Equal Employment Opportunity) matters. This results in duplication of effort—and any time two or more units are performing the same work process, misconfiguration is present.

Pay grade formulas that entail paying managers more money if they have more employees than other managers creates internal fiefdoms, self-protection, and the withholding of information. Fiefdoms quickly morph into bottlenecks and waste all kinds of time.

One of the major benefits of configuration is that it clears up a number of intractable conflicts (like fiefdoms) that, historically, have kept reappearing. These conflicts kept reappearing because they were caused by hidden misconfiguration. Misconfiguration dissipates positive energy and wears people out because, no matter what they try in order to fix the problems, nothing works. Once leaders and employees become aware of misconfiguration and its hidden costs and take steps to reconfigure the way things are done, many conflicts simply go away. Configuration "properly orders connections" within the "grid," which enables the flow of positive energy and streamlines activity.

How to Configure Your Enterprise

Headquartered in Philadelphia, HSM Consulting (pseudonym), a large executive coaching firm, had offices in twenty-six cities and was poised to grow even further. Senior executives in the firm decided that they could grow the company faster if they created a central sales department. Everyone was told that only the new sales group was responsible for generating and closing sales. Quite a few local office managers and their consultants questioned this decision but, eventually, deferred to home office. The new sales manager and her people were motivated and capable.

Unfortunately, the idea did not work. After two years, the firm's sales had dropped 23 percent and HSM's senior executives saw no evidence that things were going to get any better. Reluctantly, they disbanded the new sales department and went back to selling the firm's services the way they always had—by relying on local offices to generate and close sales. A year later, the firm's sales were up 20 percent and growing.

With all the best intentions, HSM's senior executives had misconfigured the relationship between the sales department and all of the local offices. By centralizing sales in home office, the firm's leaders had put local offices *in service to sales*. The core customer promise of HSM Consulting was customized. The local offices, their managers, and consultants were the core of the business. Salespeople needed to function in service to them, not vice versa. Each prospective client needed to learn about the consultant with whom he or she would be working and make a judgment about whether or not to go ahead with that consultant. The salespeople were just interfering with the prospect's ability to make that judgment.

To configure your enterprise, take these three steps:

- Determine what work processes must be in the core.
- Determine what work processes must be in support to the core.
- Ensure that your support units are functioning in service to the core.

Work processes that belong in the core are those that deliver directly on your customer promise. If you don't do them, you are out of business. Core work processes cannot be outsourced. Support work processes can. Step one entails sitting down with your fellow leaders and deciding what work processes must be in the core. If it cannot be outsourced, it belongs in the core. Step two is deciding if a work process can be outsourced and, if it can, it belongs in a support unit. Step three entails each support unit sitting down with the core and asking the core what it needs from that support unit. The core clarifies its goals and tells each support unit what exact *output* it needs from the support unit. *How* each support unit accomplishes the provision of that output is up to the support unit. The final decision about whether or not that output is satisfactory belongs to the core.

Each of the four living enterprises has its own particular core and template for how the core works. In a predictable and dependable enterprise, the core is operations and operational goal attainment—an electric utility's core is composed of the work processes required to harness and deliver electricity to its customers. In a best-in-class enterprise, the core is expertise and conceptual goal attainment—a surgical equipment company won't exist without its technical expertise in equipment design and manufacturing. In an enrichment enterprise, the core is value-centered goal attainment—if you value building homes for the homeless, you need the work processes required to build the homes. In a customized enterprise, the core is knowledgeable relationship goal attainment—if you are an executive coaching company, you need knowledgeable coaches who can build close relationships with customers and help them develop.

Customer demand time is a major shaping force for work processes in both the core and the support units. Customer demand for the two actuality enterprises (customized and predictable and dependable) is immediate. Customer demand for the two "possibility" enterprises (enrichment and best-in-class) emerges over time. Immediate demand (electricity, water, cars on the dealership floor, etc.) means that core work processes need to function and work with one another in certain ways. Support units need to provide what the core needs when the core needs it—as immediately as possible. Emergent demand (child development, one-of-a-kind watches) means that core has the time to do things "right." With emergent-demand cores, support units have more time and provide what the core needs in each step of the building process.

HSM Consulting did not need an in-house sales department at all. The firm could have contracted with a sales training company to provide local office consultants with more knowledge about the sales process itself. Given HSM's customized core promise and the immediacy of HSM's client demands, this outside sales training firm would be the most effective if it provided its training content and methods in real time with each consultant (e.g., mentoring the consultant in actual sales meetings with prospects—or soon thereafter).

Every time this core and support distinction is brought to the fore it causes heartaches. People who are working in a support unit interpret "support" as subservient to or as a second-class citizen. People start lobbying that "their" work unit should be in the core. This is human nature. Often, the issue is really a fear and ego issue, but people don't want to admit that. Configuration is not a covert attempt to create some kind of class hierarchy within your enterprise. Core and support are equally important. Both need one another. Configuration is simply building your "grid." Your properly connected grid allows for the efficient and timely flow of positive energy and power. Configuration is a major underpinning for system *and individual* success. Misconfiguration puts both the system and individuals in jeopardy.

Focus and configuration are the first major elements of a system-centric mind-set, and both show the perils of an individual-centric mind-set. The other major elements of a system-centric mindset are described in the next three chapters. Common to them all is the idea that if it's not good for the hive, it's not good for the bee. The hive and the bee are *both* important. Pitting them against one another is creating a false dichotomy. In every living system, it is the nature of the *connection* between the two that matters. But, you have to *start with* the hive. If you start with the bee and insist that the hive adapt to it, you put yourself and all the other bees in jeopardy. The simple, but not easy, solution is to build by starting with the hive. The bee succeeds by adapting to the hive. Our founding fathers started with the Constitution (hive), not with what was in it for each of them as individuals. The sacrifices that they made to build the "hive" are humbling, to say the least. The Constitution that they built and gave us is a miracle of history. It is the foundation of our society, a social contract, and has empowered our country and each one of us as individuals.

9

INTEGRATION

Linking the Fifteen Drivers of Culture and the Three Drivers of Leadership to Your Unique Customer Promise

➤ ➤ ➤

The assistant city manager of Tyler (pseudonym) insisted that Rob Wilkerson, utility director of Tyler Water, implement the "inverted pyramid" approach to management. Rob thought it was a terrible idea, but the city manager said the utility's hierarchical leadership was passé: "The only way for any organization to operate is to lead with teams and to decide by consensus." Inverted pyramid leadership is the opposite of hierarchical leadership. Leaders are placed at the "bottom" of the pyramid and teams of employees are placed at the "top." These teams make decisions by consensus. Managers are only supposed to ask employees what they need to accomplish a task and get them the resources. Effective leaders rely on their employees to achieve enterprise goals.

So, Rob and his leadership team went to the bottom of the pyramid and eighteen self-directed teams—one with over twenty-one members—went to the top. Two years later, after two serious accidents and five citations for regulatory violations, everyone at the utility was frustrated—especially Rob. Even though he had been against the idea from the start and all his dire predictions had come true, the board held him and his fellow leaders responsible for the mess.

Consensus decision-making fits a customized enterprise, not a predictable and dependable one like Tyler Water. The Tyler community expects clean water, 365/24/7—so equipment must be continually tested, operations tightly controlled, and decision-making based on facts and data. In a predictable and dependable enterprise, teams are composed only of the exact functions needed to gather the facts, discuss, and decide using those facts. Typically, cross-functional teams take on specific projects, accomplish specific goals, and, then, disband. If only leaders higher up have the enterprise-wide facts and information to ensure that operations stay in control, the higher-ups decide.

So, no surprise, the "inverted pyramid" didn't work for Tyler. It was the wrong organizational structure for the enterprise type. It was also the wrong way to decide, team, and lead, and to practice the cultural drivers discussed in this chapter. When it was abandoned and the properly ordered hierarchy for the enterprise type was put back in place, Tyler Water's problems went away. All enterprises need organizational structure (a cultural driver), but how structure is practiced differs by type. Customized enterprises need unique customer-focused teams and team leaders; predictable and dependable enterprises need a hierarchy; enrichment enterprises need fluid structures, and best-in-class enterprises need matrix structures.

IN THIS CHAPTER, YOU WILL LEARN:

- What Integration means
- How to integrate your enterprise
- Why integration is important
- Signs that your enterprise is not integrated

What Integration Means

Tony Hsieh, the CEO of Zappos, decided in 2014 to get rid of bosses altogether and to implement a new system of leadership and management called Holacracy. Holacracy was developed by Brian Robertson, a software engineer, and his team at Ternary Software, a Philadelphia start-up. It is a self-management process composed entirely of a plethora of teams. There is no hierarchy. There are no assigned functions or titles. Everything is decided by team judgment. No one reports to anyone. The company is entirely composed of 500 "circles" (aka teams). Some number of these circles are "on top of" other circles. Meetings abound. There are "tactical" meetings and "governance" meetings. Circles have a myriad of names attached to them.

Each meeting has a facilitator. Those in the meeting create the agenda; agenda items are called "tensions." Compensation is based on how many "badges" someone has. Badges have "people points," and if you don't have enough of these points, you are moved to a room where someone asks why you have lost your passion for the work.

For the first two years, Zappos was high on *Fortune's* Best Companies to Work For list. But now, near its third anniversary year (2016), it has fallen on forty-eight of fifty-eight measures and is close to being taken off the list. Almost 30 percent of its staff has turned over. Holacracy has created chaos and uncertainty. People are not sure what the company stands for, and many feel things are out of control.

In the framework of this book, CEO Hsieh has created a collaboration culture, albeit an odd one. It is difficult to come up with a definition of the company's leadership approach, except to say that it appears that everyone is a leader. CEO Hsieh's entrepreneurial spirit is quite admirable, and it appears to have paid off for him—Zappos was purchased by Amazon in 2009 and Hsieh received a very large sum of money for his Zappos shares. However, there are several major disconnections going on here. For one, everything points to the great likelihood that Zappos is a predictable and dependable enterprise. It is essentially an online catalog of items for purchase. Products are not tailored to the specifics of each customer who buys an item online—which would call for a collaboration culture and participative leadership. Zappos's major promise is that the customer has a convenient way to buy and receive an item in its catalog (shipping is free). A predictable and dependable promise calls for a control culture and directive leadership, not a collaboration culture and some brand of participative leadership.

CEO Hsieh has abandoned the very culture and leadership that he needs. There are quite a few ways to operate a control culture and engage in directive leadership that are humane, fun, and empowering. Zappos's customers are probably receiving what they were promised, but it is all happening *in spite of* Hsieh's Holacracy. It is likely, though, that the contradictions will slowly undermine his intentions. Holacracy appears to be a case of "no more bosses around here because I said so." There is still a definite demand for Zappos's products, so that should keep the revenues coming in, but even if they continue to come in, Holacracy will add unnecessary costs to the company's P&L.

Integration means that the enterprises' (or unit's) culture and leadership drivers are practiced consistently with the enterprise's (or unit's) customer promise. Each of the four living enterprises *practice* culture and leadership differently. Chapters 2–5 describe each living enterprise and the exact cultural and leadership practices that work for each; these drivers are also listed and briefly described in Chapter 1.

Integration illustrates the important distinction between principles and practices. The same principles apply to all four enterprises. All four need to set clear direction, make effective decisions, manage performance effectively, provide organizational structure, team effectively, etc. But, each enterprise practices these same principles differently, which is where integration comes into play.

Cultural and leadership practices are based on your customer promise and what it takes for your enterprise to deliver on that promise. Put another way, cultural and leadership practices are based on what it takes to succeed in your marketplace. They should not be based on some amalgamation of individual values, the opposite of some CEO's unpleasant early experiences with a particular leadership approach, deeply held individual assumptions, or people's needs to have fun or work in a relaxing environment. They should not be based on "big data," electronic monitoring of employee walking patterns, communication patterns, informal conversations in the company kitchen, or rites and rituals.

Cultural and leadership practices should be based on what your living people system *must do to deliver on its customer promise.* What many people call "culture" is actually the behavioral science concept of "climate," meaning "how things *feel* around here."

Holacracy at Zappos comes from an individual-centric mind-set. Paradoxically, individuals are happier in a system-centric enterprise. When an organization builds and implements an integrated system, individuals are much more engaged and effective because their work has a greater chance of succeeding and they know that. Staying locked into the individual-centric mindset dis-integrates the enterprise and diminishes the chances that individual acts will have successful effects.

In Zappos's third year of Holacracy, 30 percent of the employees have turned over, people are confused about where the company is going, and the fortunes of the company are turning down. Hsieh hated rules and bureaucracy, so he created a free and open enterprise that is filled with rules. Zappos appears to be a collective of individuals desperate for a system. People are flailing about trying to preserve individual freedom in a vacuum.

Unfortunately, the whole enterprise is structured around Hsieh's individual-centric vision. He seems to believe that a working system will spring from within the minds and hearts of 2,000 individual people who move in and out of 500 circles. In effect, Hsieh appears to believe that if he can set things up at Zappos to create 2,000 entrepreneurs just like himself, the company will do well.

How to Integrate Your Enterprise

Benson Public Relations (BPR) (pseudonym) is a 110-person public relations firm that had come upon hard times. Revenues and profitability were down and key employees were leaving. Customer complaints were increasing at an alarming rate.

The firm's difficulties began about a year after the firm's chief operating officer (COO), a woman who had worked in this capacity for twenty-five years, retired. With her and the CEO's leadership, the firm grew, it was profitable, and customers were very happy with its services. For twenty-five years, BPR's CEO had left the day-to-day work of the firm to her COO. When the COO left, however, the CEO decided to run the firm by herself. Up to that point, the CEO had devoted all of her time to marketing, sales, and customer acquisition, while the COO managed day-to-day delivery of BPR's public relations services.

The administration of our analytics showed that leaders and employees saw customer promise as *customized*, core culture as *collaborative*, and core leadership as *both participative and standard setter*. When it came to culture drivers, they saw:

- Nature and use of power and role of employee as collaboration and competence
- Managing conflict as competence
- Decision-making, managing performance, promotion, information technology, hiring, and managing change as un-categorized
- Organizational structure, nature of work, compensation, teaming, and managing innovation as collaboration
- People development as cultivation

When it came to leadership drivers, they saw:

- Set direction as participative
- Mobilize commitment as standard setter
- Build organizational capability as unclear

Most public relations firms are customized enterprises. Their business is building a close partnership with each unique customer, gaining a thorough picture of each customer's business and current presence in the marketplace, and customizing a tailored PR campaign for each. BPR's core customer promise result—customized—is consistent with expectations. People within the firm are clear about BPR's customer promise.

The core culture is experienced as collaboration, which is the integrated (properly connected) core culture for a customized enterprise. Culture driver results are revealing, in that power in the firm is a 50-50 mixture of collaboration and competence—diametric opposites of one another. This has to be having a deleterious effect on productivity because these two ways to practice power cancel one another out. The practice of decision-making and managing performance is inconsistent and confusing to people. Oddly, the nature of work and teaming are experienced as collaboration, but role of employee is a mixture of collaboration and competence. For some reason, people experience the work itself as collaborative and team-based, but not their individual roles. The problematic combining of collaboration and competence practices shows up again and is further reinforced by the core leadership (overall firm leaders as a group) results and the leadership driver's results—a mixture of participative and standard setter. For all practical purposes, the firm is split down the middle when it comes to leadership.

Culture and leadership results pointed in the direction of the firm's CEO and COO changes as the likely root cause of the firm's difficulties. The CEO and COO both completed our individual leader assessment (the former COO agreed to come back and complete the assessment) and the results saw the CEO's leadership approach as standard setter and the COO's leadership approach as participative.

These individual leadership results are quite instructive. What we see is that the former COO was a strong participative leader. Her leadership approach was integrated with the core customer promise and core culture of BPR. However, when the CEO, a strong standard-setter leader, took over COO responsibilities and continued to function as the primary salesperson for the firm, things started to go awry. With all the best intentions, when the CEO took over the COO's job as well, she began leading the firm in an un-integrated manner. For quite a while, she was unconsciously (and unintentionally) pulling the firm off center, confusing employees and customers, and diminishing operational and financial performance. The fact that she was the CEO only compounded the issue because people were reluctant to confront her. Additionally, the firm had been doing quite well under her CEO leadership (when the COO was around).

As a result of these insights, BPR decided to:

- Limit the CEO's role to what it had been before the COO retired.
- Reinstitute the COO position and fill it with a participative leader. Allow the COO to run the business, day-to-day.
- Ensure that decisions are made by consensus and that managing performance is based on PR campaign success and customer satisfaction.
- Clarify for employees that their role is essentially to contribute to the unique success of each customer by fully participating in team processes. Individual expertise needs to be channeled into what each unique customer needs and can afford.

Two years later, this firm had completely recovered. Revenues and profits were up 38 percent and 31 percent, respectively. Employees were much more productive. Key employees stayed with the firm and customer complaints stopped.

Integrating your enterprise is a matter of properly ordering your fifteen culture drivers and your three leadership drivers. It is important to know which ones are already integrated and which ones are not. The integrated drivers are strengths to be built upon. It works best if you start with the unintegrated drivers that have the most impact—leadership, decision-making, compensation, performance management, nature and use of power, and nature of work. Leaders and employees readily embrace making these changes because they address the root causes of what is holding them back from winning in the marketplace and what they need to do differently in order to lose less and win more. Every individual wins when the system wins. The key is to identify the root causes of *system* disconnections and then implement the properly ordered connections required by your customer promise.

The work of Kurt Lewin provides a simple, but effective, framework for implementing integration. Lewin proposed that for a living system to be effective it must possess a high degree of freedom. If the system is stuck, it must focus on increasing the system's degree of freedom. Leaders and employees need to help the system "unfreeze" by identifying the forces that are driving movement toward a goal and the forces that are hindering that movement. This is very close to what I am talking about when I say "create conditions for success." Properly ordered connections drive movement toward the goal and disconnections hinder movement toward the goal. Properly ordered connections "unfreeze" and empower your enterprise.

This notion of "unfreezing" led Lewin to come up with his idea of "force field analysis," which is depicted in Figure 9-1. The way to integrate your enterprise is to conduct a "force field analysis."

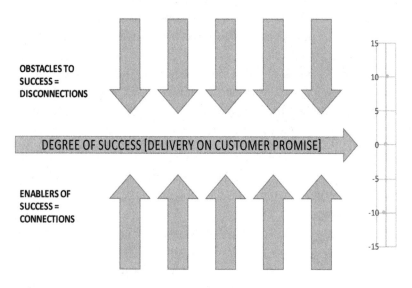

Figure 9-1. Lewin's Force Field Analysis

Why Integration Is Important

Between 40 and 50 percent of elementary and secondary school teachers leave their profession by the end of the fifth year of their starting their career. Local, state, and federal governments are operating from a one-size-fits-all mentality that is more appropriate to an assembly line or factory (part of a predictable and dependable enterprise) than to the classroom (part of an enrichment enterprise).

Our centralized, data-driven, standardized, and test-driven educational system mechanizes students and teachers. There is a nationwide backlash from teachers, students, and parents who are sick of over-testing. Students in big-city schools will take, on average, 112 mandatory standardized tests between prekindergarten and high school graduation—that translates into 8 tests a year. There is a long list of federal mandates that put high stakes on student test results. Test results now are being used to determine pay for teachers and federal funding for school districts. This has led to schools giving students dozens of additional tests to prepare for the federal tests. One county school district in Florida gave more than 242 standardized tests to its students between kindergarten and their high school graduation. Only 17 of those were federally required. In early 2015, Arizona state superintendent Diane Douglas called on the governor to defy federal law by opting out of an entire set of required exams. "Stop this madness and put our children first," she said.

Teachers are no longer allowed to develop their own methods for evaluating how well their students are learning and developing. Teachers and students are regimented to the minute. Teachers are barred from differentiating instruction, are required to complete forms that have little or nothing to do with development, and are forced into a system that effectively depersonalizes their students in their most formative years.

Arne Duncan, former U.S. secretary of education, says that there is "no question that we need to check at least once a year to make sure our kids are on track." Washington believes that higher expectations and accountability will "lift the performance" of American students. Our federal government spends approximately $79 billion annually on elementary and secondary education programs in the states.

Our elementary and secondary public school system is the mother of all dis-integrations! Elementary and secondary schools are enrichment enterprises. Their customer promise is to help our children learn and develop, to have fuller lives, and to fulfill their potential. Our schools are about people possibilities. Decision-making needs to be *personal*. Power should be value (belief) based. Teacher's *judgment* must be the basis for delivering on the customer promise of our schools. Our schools are flower gardens. Flowers come in all colors, sizes, and shapes. Some grow fast, some grow slowly. Flowers need to be nurtured, watered, and protected.

The factors that impinge upon the development of our children are myriad—socioeconomic, racial, geographic, political, familial, among others. Teachers need to make judgments about the education of each and every child in their school while taking all these factors into account. Some children are more ready to learn than others. Some are more mature than others. Students learn differently from one another.

But in the United States, federal, state, and local governments try to lead and control what goes on in the classroom. Our schools are not predictable and dependable enterprises. Enrichment and predictable and dependable are diametric opposites of one another. Centralized and standardized testing is a practice of an actuality/impersonal (predictable and dependable) enterprise. Testing measures *information exchange*, pure and simple. That is fine, as far as it goes. Testing does have a role to play in our schools. Test results are a particular source of information. Given the enormity of what it takes to educate our children and the sophisticated judgment-making needed from our teachers to assess their progress, test scores are a drop in the ocean. Tying school system funding and teacher performance and pay to test scores seriously damages the development and growth of our children. Are electronic badges and monitors around students' and teachers' necks and bodies next? You cannot centrally control an emergent process (child education and development) from on high. You can only catalyze it. Secretary Duncan's mandate to "make sure our kids are on track" and Washington's belief that we can "lift the performance" of American students make no sense. "On track" to what? How do you "lift" the growth of a flower?

Until we integrate the customer promise of elementary and secondary education with the right culture and leadership approach, we will remain stuck in place, squander many of our children's lives, and waste billions of our tax dollars.

Integration is important because we make the greatest gains when it is present and pay the biggest costs when it is lacking. The fifteen culture drivers and three leadership drivers, separately, entirely, or partly, either enable your success in the marketplace or block it. The more your enterprise is integrated, the more effective your strategy implementation is and the more your people are unified. People are more efficient, free, and engaged. Goals are met and positive energy flows. People see themselves and the enterprise winning.

Integration provides a template and roadmap for *behavior*. The actual practices [behaviors] required for each of the fifteen culture drivers and three leadership drivers are spelled out for each living enterprise in Chapters 2–5.) As soon as Tyler Water "inverted the pyramid" back to where it belonged, we trained leaders, managers, and supervisors in directive leadership, with particular emphasis on the mobilizing commitment leadership driver. Then people understood what they needed to do and how to do it. This will always be the result when you let integration describe and determine behavior. Integration takes things from the realm of theory to practical action. It keeps everyone headed in the same direction and out of rabbit holes. Productivity greatly improves, so integration saves energy, wasted time and effort, and money.

Signs That Your Enterprise Is Not Integrated

The HR software market is booming. As of August 2016, it was a $14 billion marketplace. When it comes to HR processes, you name it and someone is already technologizing it, automating it, and selling it. Consultants, software engineers, financiers, MBAs, and other kinds of vendors are mechanizing and monetizing people at a furious pace. We are in the new age of the quantified customer, the quantified employee, and the quantified leader. Leaders and managers at their keyboards now have software available that allows them to: recruit, train, develop, hire, onboard, track, pay, appraise the performance of, enculturate, engage, empower, build teams of, retain, structure, improve the wellness and fitness of, take the pulse (how happy or unhappy) of, get feedback from, gamify, entertain, reduce the boredom of, find a place to sit for, create badges and trophies and credits for, help plan vacations for, and manage personal expenses for their people.

The look and feel of all this technology is following the broader world of technology, particularly social media technology. Menus, dropdowns, tables, panels, or dashboards are on the way out. Now everyone can swipe, punch, scan, and scroll. Sensors are coming that will tell us and our managers where we are, how many steps we took, what our voice sounds like, our heartbeats, how we feel, and how we are breathing. We can now use information about employee tone of voice and motion to understand what causes stress at work, create a "mood meter" to help employees rearrange their offices, make meetings better, and identify leadership behaviors that improve engagement. These tools can coach you on management and leadership style, determine how well you possess "competencies," help you stay relaxed and fit at work, rate the usefulness of meetings, and set team goals. "Behavioral economics" have appeared. Now there is no more "telling" your employees to do anything. Telling is out, and suggesting is in. Only "nudges," are allowed. "Directives" are no longer permitted.

By latest count, there are approximately sixty-four companies in the HR software business. Hats off to "big data"!

So, what exactly do we have here? Are we on the verge of an exciting new era of innovation and change? The next "giant step for mankind"? Is this a new kind of "Moore's Law," where the number of transistors in a dense integrated circuit doubles approximately every two years? Have we been able to take all of the work done in the areas of customer satisfaction, culture, and leadership in the last hundred years and boil it all down to software technology (cram it all into a "dense integrated circuit")? There is now a software tool that can measure the culture of your enterprise in "seven minutes." One of the founders of this company (a software engineer) claims that "all you need to know about when it comes to culture are these thirty-six values." If seven minutes is too long, there is another vendor that has a "Culture Quiz" that "identifies the culture traits that matter most to your organization" in only three minutes! And, when you are done with the "quiz," they will award you and your enterprise with one or more of seven "badges." Culture analysis in three minutes! Really? Leadership development on your smartphone in seven minutes! Really? If you get the founders of all sixty-four HR software businesses in the room and ask them how they feel about central control in profit and nonprofit enterprises, most will decry it. But, if you step back and look at what they are selling with their information technology, software, and "platforms," they are selling central control!

Information technology (IT) has a useful role to play in the conduct of free enterprise. It is one of the fifteen culture drivers delineated in this book. It is not, however, alive. It is not one of the elements of your living people system (network). It is a medium of information exchange and should be practiced differently in each one of the four enterprises. It is a "tail." It is not the "dog." It has to be used *in service to* people, not vice versa. There is no value in attempting to technologize people. Trying to technologize people is dis-integrating, not integrating. It is a form of technological reductionism that primarily results in taking your enterprise off center and interfering with your ability to deliver on your customer promise.

It is textbook fad-ism. Fads are sure signs of dis-integration. Running your enterprise by putting big data front and center has many unfortunate consequences. The major ones are the mechanization of people, another brand of central control, increased turnover among leaders and employees, and the injection of quite a number of crosscurrents and contradictions into the enterprise. The big negative consequence is that big data takes the life out of your enterprise. It's "unreal."

Other signs that your enterprise is not integrated are endless meetings that lead nowhere, leaders taking their differences with one another into the work activities of their employees, inefficient activities, wasted time, mixed messages from leaders, unresolved conflicts, problems that keep reappearing, many hidden agendas, people frustrated and demoralized, left hands not knowing what right hands are doing, high level of employee and/or leader turnover, and many people refusing to take responsibility for actions.

When it comes to leading your living people system and building a lasting enterprise, there are no quick silver bullets. Integrating your enterprise takes time. You can't do it in three or seven minutes. The benefits of integration are that it identifies root causes of problems that keep reappearing (because those causes were never addressed) and removes them. By understanding the root causes of what is happening in your enterprise and building on the culture and leadership drivers that fit your kind of enterprise you improve effectiveness by *building* the *system* that delivers on your customer promise. The drivers are your building blocks. You just need to know which ones are already in place and which ones need to be practiced differently and how to do it. Once you do, you'll be out of the individual blame business and into the integration business—and freeing up everyone in your enterprise. Ironically, that happens not in loose and unmoored organizations like Zappos but in integrated systems like BPR's, after it integrated itself and unfroze.

10

BALANCE
Keeping Your Strengths from Becoming Weaknesses

➤ ➤ ➤

The space shuttle *Challenger* took off from Cape Canaveral, Florida, on January 28, 1986, an unusually cold day. Seventy-three seconds into flight, it disintegrated, killing all seven crewmembers.

This disaster resulted in a thirty-two-month hiatus in the shuttle program and the formation of the Rogers Commission, a special commission appointed by President Reagan to investigate the accident. After extensive analysis, the commission concluded that the direct cause of the accident was a faulty O-ring seal in the shuttle's right solid rocket booster (SRB), but the primary cause of the accident was the culture and leadership of Morton Thiokol and NASA itself. NASA managers had known since 1977 that contractor Morton Thiokol's design of the O-ring seal was faulty.

The SRB contained a potentially catastrophic flaw in the O-rings, but they had sat on this information because NASA's leaders had created a culture of "don't bring us bad news." They also disregarded warnings from engineers about the dangers of launching posed by the low temperatures that morning and failed to adequately report these technical concerns to their superiors.

NASA is a predictable and dependable enterprise. It needs a hierarchy. But, when leaders go too far and over-control subordinates, the enterprise gets out of balance: Decision-making power becomes overly top-down and leaders ignore messages from below. These leaders also tend to inundate people below with data and information without giving them any way of knowing what is important and what isn't. Every enterprise's strengths taken to an extreme turn into weaknesses. This never ends well: Unaddressed, these weakness can cause the kind of failure that occurred with the *Challenger* launch.

A balanced enterprise is functioning in a state of equilibrium. Integrated culture and leadership drivers are being practiced appropriately and not taken to extremes. To predict how an enterprise will get out of balance, look at the principles of its opposite type. Typically, a predictable and dependable enterprise will get into trouble when it comes to the principles of the enrichment enterprise. A central principle of an enrichment enterprise is to fully enable its people to contribute and to encourage their ideas, whatever they may be. An out-of-balance predictable and dependable enterprise will do the opposite: get over-controlling and stifle input from people. Conversely, an out-of-balance enrichment enterprise will overly value intentionality and undervalue controls and structure. An out-of-balance best-in-class enterprise will, predictably, have difficulty with teaming, and an out-of-balance customized enterprise will have difficulty with individual expertise.

A balanced enterprise practices, as fully as possible, the principles of the culture and leadership *opposite* to its core culture and core leadership. It does not mean practicing the *practices* of its opposite culture and leadership. It means practicing the *principles* of its opposite kind of enterprise. If a best-in-class enterprise gets too individualistic and doesn't team as much as advised, it should practice teaming in a way that fits a best-in-class enterprise—build project teams that have the necessary experts to accomplish specified goals.

IN THIS CHAPTER, YOU WILL LEARN:

- Why balance is important
- How to tell if your enterprise is out of balance
- How to balance your enterprise

Why Balance Is Important

In 1992, Nokia came out with the Nokia 1011, the first commercial mobile phone. By 1998, Nokia was the bestselling mobile phone brand.

By 2008, the mobile and smartphone market was ablaze, and major competitors were growing fast. Nokia's Symbian platform for its smartphones was quickly becoming outdated. The iPhone OS and Android platforms were much more successful. Nokia sold its phone business to Microsoft in 2014.

So, what happened to Nokia and its smartphone business? Why did the business fail? First, Nokia senior leadership decided to evolve the company into a conglomerate—mostly by way of acquisition. It acquired businesses in the following sectors: services (imaging apps, navigation apps, developer tools, websites, video gaming), security, tablets, modems, televisions, telephone switches, military communications, personal computers, computer displays, and others. Second, the company and its leadership got way out of balance.

Nokia's senior leaders wanted a very big company and needed a high stock price and a lot of cash to bring that about. Consequently, they put the pressure on and created a culture of fear. The message throughout the company was: perform, perform, perform; generate as much cash as possible; and push Nokia's stock price up. Senior leaders regularly shouted at people at the top of their lungs and threatened to fire or demote middle managers. Middle managers quickly got the message that they should not tell senior leaders bad news.

For example, middle managers knew that the Symbian platform was way behind Apple's OS and Alphabet's (at the time named Google) Android. But that was, definitely, not something senior leaders wanted to hear. So, they didn't tell them. Only positive, optimistic information flowed up to senior leaders. Basically, middle managers lied to them so that they could keep their jobs. Middle managers wanted to hold on to as much power as they could and created silos because they were afraid that their resources would be allocated elsewhere and they would be demoted or fired. This created a vicious cycle—given the optimistic messages coming from middle managers, senior leaders had no qualms about pushing them harder to catch up and go beyond the competition. This created more fear. Senior leaders wanted everything monetized (predicted revenues, costs, profits, etc.), which, in effect, turned engineers into faux financiers who just started telling people above them what they wanted to hear.

Nokia's senior leaders took their power to an extreme and turned it from a strength into a weakness. They also took the strength that they needed—the company's middle managers and its engineers—and turned them into a weakness by disempowering them. By muscling them, senior leaders turned their key resources into liars and the lies caused these senior leaders to make hugely detrimental decisions that almost put the company under.

Balance keeps your enterprise from operating in extremes. Nokia's leaders took their definitiveness and proactive exercise of authority too far and became autocratic. This drove their people into hiding, self-protection, and eventually lying. Their lying created misinformation for senior leadership and led to even worse outcomes—particularly poor decision-making that had major financial and other deleterious effects on their enterprise. Before they sold their smartphone business to Microsoft, they were on the verge of bankruptcy. If, instead, the company's leaders hadn't gone to such extremes (over-controlling, over-emphasizing profit and performance), people below them would have been straight with them and helped them keep the company out of trouble.

Balance keeps your enterprise disciplined and fit. It steadies your enterprise and keeps it stable. It is like guiding a sailboat through wind and water. If you lean too far, you are prone toward tipping over. Equilibrium literally means a state of balance due to the equal action of opposing forces. It keeps you centered.

Taking things to the extreme is a natural, almost universal, human tendency. Your enterprise *will* get out of balance—to one degree or another. Things can, and will, go wrong. Pressures will emerge, both from within and without. Conflict is inevitable. "Opposing forces" are ever-present. Because conflict is seen as bad, people go to extremes to keep it from happening or try to quash it right away. But conflict is *simply negative feedback*. It is quite important because it tells you what is *not working*. Positive and negative feedback are both essential because they give you the information that you need in order to maintain your progress. You need both to effectively guide your sailboat ahead.

Because so many people are averse to conflict, their emotions understandably take over when it arises—they try to ignore it or do something that will "make it" disappear. This issue can compound when people and their enterprise are successful, which is why success so often contains the seeds of failure. It can breed a false sense of immunity, which, then, breeds complacency and single-mindedness. In an enterprise, that creates trouble *for the system*. Some individuals may escape the consequences, but the system will become vulnerable.

Balance is hard work and requires discipline, and it is vital to your enterprise. It keeps opposing forces (conflicts) connected so that solutions can be co-developed. Balance is another kind of connection. Nokia's senior leaders broke the connection with their own middle managers and engineers. Without balance, your enterprise loses resourcefulness and flexibility. Imbalance will take you off course. It destabilizes your system.

Walmart tracks its workers' comings and goings by their barcodes. To call in sick, workers must dial a 1-800 number, identify themselves by their eight-digit birthday, the last four digits of their social security number, and their four-digit store number followed by the pound key, and then press 1 to indicate that they are calling to report an absence, 1 to indicate that the absence is for today, any number 1–5 for reasons ranging from personal illness to natural disaster, only to get a ten-digit confirmation number and be re-routed to their store, where they are expected to speak with a salaried member of management before getting off the line, itself a process that can take upwards of twenty minutes.

This example of out-of-balance leadership and culture is not something that will put Walmart out of business. But, here is what it does do. It mechanizes the company's employees. It disconnects employees and leaders. Leaders treat their employees as objects that can be barcoded, just like their products. Employees lose trust in their leaders and objectify them back.

Other inferences aside, this is a practical problem for the company. It diminishes Walmart's strength and resourcefulness. And the costs of that far outweigh whatever benefit leadership sees in this procedure. Mechanizing all of your employees creates considerable negative energy, which spreads throughout the enterprise. That discolors the attitudes of both leaders and employees. These chickens will come home to roost every day, throughout the company. More people will leave. More work will be duplicated. Employees will do only what they have to do to keep their jobs. Employees will "delegate up" work to their leaders as much as they can. Walmart's annual turnover among its hourly employees is 44 percent—almost half, every year. *Harvard Business Review* estimates that for skilled and semi-skilled jobs, the fully loaded cost of replacing a worker who leaves is typically 1.5 to 2.5 times the worker's annual salary. Obviously, these workers are leaving for additional reasons (notably, low pay). But, why make the problem worse? Do you think barcoding employees fosters turnover or reduces it? Barcoding and mechanizing employees is taking system control and letting it spill over into people control. Keeping the system in control is a strength. Applying it to employee control is taking it too far and turns it into a weakness.

Signs That Your Enterprise Is Out of Balance

When workers at Amazon's warehouses first show up to clock in they are given the daily report of employee theft. The report provides the stories of co-workers fired for theft. Amazon discourages stealing by putting up flat-screen TVs that display examples of alleged on-the-job theft. The alleged offenders are not identified by name. Each is represented by a black silhouette stamped with the word terminated and accompanied by details such as when they stole, what they stole, how much it was worth, and how they got caught. Some of the silhouettes are marked arrested. For warehouses that don't have flat-screens, tales of firings are posted on sheets of paper tacked to bulletin boards or taped to the wall.

Amazon also uses monitoring technologies to track the minute-by-minute movements and performance of employees. At each warehouse Amazon tags its employees with personal satellite navigation computers that tell employees the route they must travel to shelve consignments of goods, sets target times for their warehouse journeys, and then measure whether targets are met. All of this information is available to management in real time, and if an employee is behind schedule, he will receive a text message pointing this out and telling him to reach his targets or suffer the consequences. This monitoring reveals minute-by-minute movements of each employee. In addition, six people called "co-workers" and "leads" on each packing line keep the packing line moving. They reprimand employees for speaking to one another or for pausing too long. They record how often the packers go to the bathroom and, if they don't go to the bathroom closest to their line, they want to know why they did that.

Amazon has the second highest turnover of any Fortune 500 company. Average employee tenure is just one year. Amazon is taking its technology strength and turning it into a weakness. Surely the cost to replace the majority of its employees every year has to far exceed the benefit of running the warehouses this way. Coming up with a way to operate warehouses less extremely before the robots get there has to be a possibility.

Employee turnover is a sign of imbalance. Because a strength taken to an extreme becoming a weakness is not an idea most people understand, the weakness persists or it gets "treated" in some way or another that does not work (because the root cause is not being addressed). When imbalances are unattended to, the negative effects spread out and create more problems. In the case of Nokia's smartphone, the imbalance led to misinformation that almost put the company out of business.

The thing about imbalance is that it is built in—because it comes from our strengths. Taking one's strengths to an extreme is simply human nature. Therefore, the signs of where *your* imbalance is highly likely to appear are contained in the central principles of the living enterprise *opposite* to yours. This fact gives you a heads-up on what to watch out for. Figures 10-1 through 10-4 contain a summary of the central principles of each of the four living enterprises and the likely kinds of imbalance for each.

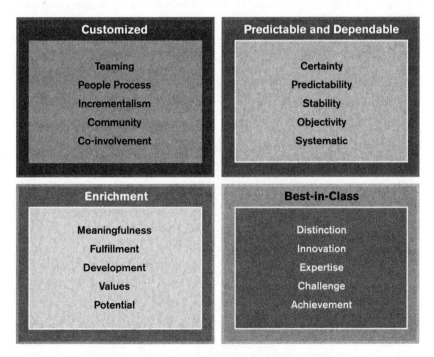

Customized	Predictable and Dependable
Teaming	Certainty
People Process	Predictability
Incrementalism	Stability
Community	Objectivity
Co-involvement	Systematic

Enrichment	Best-in-Class
Meaningfulness	Distinction
Fulfillment	Innovation
Development	Expertise
Values	Challenge
Potential	Achievement

Figure 10-1. Summary of Central Principles of the Four Living Enterprises—Culture

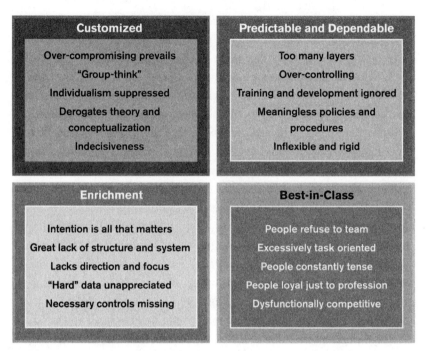

Figure 10-2. Summary of Likely Imbalance of the Four Living Enterprises—Culture

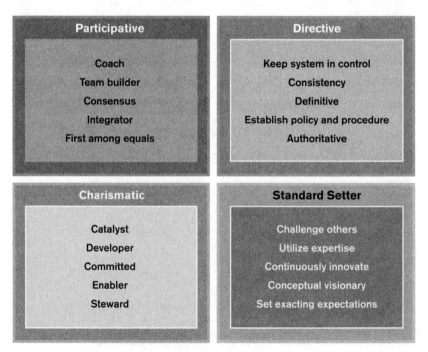

Figure 10-3. Summary of Central Principles of the Four Living Enterprises—Leadership

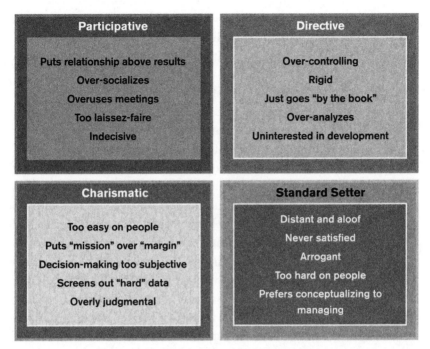

Figure 10-4. Summary of Likely Imbalance of Central Principles of the
Four Living Enterprises–Leadership

For example, an enrichment enterprise will resist controls. The predictable and dependable enterprise will neglect the development of its people. The customized enterprise will have a hard time dealing with conceptualizers. The best-in-class enterprise will struggle with teaming.

How to Balance Your Enterprise

The USS Benfold is a $1 billion warship in the U.S. Navy's arsenal of destroyers. When Commander D. Michael Abrashoff took command of the Benfold, it was the worst performing ship in the Navy's Pacific Fleet. Its sailor retention rate was only 8 percent. It had the highest accident rates in the entire fleet. Morale was low. When the crew was told Abrashoff's predecessor was being replaced, the entire crew cheered.

Fifteen months later, the Navy rated the Benfold as the best ship in the fleet. Abrashoff's leadership approach produced benefits that were both operational and financial. The Benfold returned $600,000 of its $2.4 million maintenance budget and $800,000 of its $3 million repair budget.

He and the crew completed the navy's pre-deployment training cycle in record time: They took five days in port and fourteen days under way when most ships take twenty-two days in port and thirty days under way. On average, only 54 percent of sailors remain in the Navy after their second tour of duty. Under Abrashoff's command, 100 percent of the Benfold's career sailors signed on for an additional tour. That saved the Navy $1.6 million in personnel-related costs.

What did Commander Abrashoff do to turn the ship around?

His summary of what he did was to focus on *purpose (an enrichment principle)* rather than on chain of command. He shifted the ship's organizing principle from obedience to performance. He met with his entire crew, 300 sailors, and got to know them personally. Then, he told the crew that he wanted them to think of every process on the ship and to come up with their own ideas for how to improve them. He asked them to focus on how each idea for improvement would help them to maintain operational readiness. He did not stop at the ship's standard operating procedures (SOP). If his crew convinced him that a particular SOP was meaningless, he threw it out. He kept asking if there was a better way. He listened to his crew. He told the crew that their job was not to support *him*, it was to drive effective *performance*.

What Commander Abrashoff did is a classic example of how to balance your enterprise. The Benfold was a predictable and dependable enterprise when he took command and it was a predictable and dependable enterprise fifteen months later. However, every change he made (led in a *directive* way) was based on the principles of the predictable and dependable enterprise's opposite: the enrichment cultivation culture and charismatic leadership approach. He did not try to turn the destroyer into an enrichment enterprise. He took the principles of the enrichment culture (purpose, fulfillment, development, values, and potential) and the principles of charismatic leadership (catalyst, developer, committed, enabler, and steward) and *practiced* them in a manner consistent and properly ordered with a predictable and dependable enterprise.

He had to do this because the Benfold was way out of balance and this was the only way to get it back into balance. In the language of this book, he went to his living people system and empowered his people to be co-developers and co-controllers (with him) in order to ensure that the ship's operational system stayed in control and functioned effectively. He did not focus on controlling his people. He focused on performance of the ship's operational system and goal attainment. He did not tell his crew that the goals were financial (cost reduction, etc.). Cost reductions occurred as a result of improvements to the operational system.

He tapped into his crew's motivation to contribute to the ship's success, not by focusing on his crew's individual traits but by working on the system as a whole. He celebrated the crew's accomplishments all along the way. He focused on what was needed for the system (ship) to work and deliver on its promise. He did not focus on what individual sailors were doing "wrong." He wanted to know what was working and not working. He did not re-write job descriptions. He did not "stack rank" his sailors. *He created conditions for all of them to work together (connect) to accomplish operational system goals.* He asked the sailors to help one another out. He and his crew tracked progress together, and, when something was not working, they all worked to come up with a better way to accomplish the ship's goals. When the crew reduced the pre-deployment training cycle, he did not try to squeeze more work out of them, he gave them more shore leave. He didn't coerce his crew, he enabled them.

Balance keeps a dynamic equilibrium present within your enterprise. The way you balance your enterprise is to assume that there will be ongoing pressure to take one or more of your strengths too far, to regularly assess where imbalance is present, and to regularly take action to get your enterprise back in balance and to keep it that way.

Only you, your fellow leaders, and your people can identify where you are out-of-balance and get your enterprise back in balance. Technology won't do it. Mechanization won't do it. Setting financial goals won't do it. People get out of balance; people get you back in balance. You can't get more technologized and mechanized than the USS Benfold. Commander Abrashoff went straight to his crew to get the ship balanced. The real answer came from his *people, not technology or mechanization.*

When symptoms like low morale, high turnover, poor performance, and/or a low level of accountability appear, ask your employees and fellow leaders to tell you what is working, what is not working, what they would change, and where you as an organization are taking your strengths too far. Go over the principles of culture and leadership opposite to your enterprise and ask employees and leaders to use these as a beginning outline. Ask them to focus on the enterprise's core customer promise and the system in place to deliver on that. Decide which issues to work on and prioritize them. Establish goals, implementation plans, and timelines. Track progress. Ask people to help one another succeed. Reward progress and celebrate accomplishments. Whether symptoms appear or not, it is a good idea to address the issue of imbalance at least annually—as a form of checkup. The more imbalances can be nipped in the bud, the better.

Commander Abrashoff did all these things and some others that bear mention. He treated his crew as co-developers and co-problem-solvers. He asked his crew to be co-responsible (with him) for operating a top-notch destroyer. He listened—listening does not equate to agreeing, it equates to receiving information. He got to know his crew personally. He treated his fellow leaders and crew members as a community. He asked his crew what they thought should be added to what they were already doing—what was missing that they hadn't thought of before.

Maintaining balance is a discipline. Whether we like it or not, we will take things too far. It's just human nature. So, we need to accept that fact and build in an ongoing way to catch imbalance as soon as we can and correct it. If we let imbalance go on too long, it gets harder and harder to do something about it. Imbalance creates negative energy and a vicious cycle. Balance creates positive energy and a virtuous cycle. The key thing to remember about balance is that the potential to get out of balance is always present within your enterprise. Rather than lament this truism and hope it doesn't happen to you and your enterprise, it pays to proactively look for signs of it and head it off at the pass.

11

ADAPTATION

Adapting to Environmental and Life Cycle Changes

➤ ➤ ➤

When one of Kodak's engineers invented the first digital camera in 1975, the senior executives responded with: "That's cute—but don't tell anyone about it." And, for six years, Kodak ignored digital photography. In 1981, the company's market research group looked at the core technologies and likely adoption curves around silver halide film versus digital photography. The results of the study produced both bad news and good news. The bad news was that digital photography had the potential capability to replace Kodak's established film business. The good news was that it would take roughly ten years for that to occur. But Kodak did little to prepare for that; instead, it used digital photography to improve the quality of its film. Kodak filed for bankruptcy in 2012.

Things change. New products and technologies appear, new competitors come on the scene, new regulations are developed, markets shrink, and markets get saturated. This is a beginning list. Adaptation has to do with effectively responding to change. Not responding to change can stall your enterprise's growth and even put you out of business. Kodak is a classic example of a company that refused to adapt. When the research study results were in and the head of market research told leaders that Kodak had about ten years to progressively add digital photography, the company should have started making decisions and plans. Even if Kodak leaders had decided that they needed more evidence, adaptation demanded that they learn more and work to get that evidence. Adaptation tells you to stay vigilant, take nothing for granted, and continually stay open to change. Not doing that leaves you vulnerable to a situation like Kodak's.

Are you and your fellow leaders fighting to not lose instead of fighting to win? Are you complacent? Is your enterprise resting on a plateau instead of looking for new paths to climb? Then, you're not adapting. This chapter will show you how to adapt and not only survive but thrive, whatever happens.

IN THIS CHAPTER, YOU WILL LEARN:

- Why adaptation is important
- Signs that you are not adapting
- How to ensure that your enterprise continues to adapt to inevitable changes in the marketplace

Why Adaptation Is Important

In its heyday, Blockbuster, the video-rental company, had more than 50 million customers worldwide. By 1989, Blockbuster was opening a new store every seventeen hours. In England, the company opened 1,000 stores in one year. But, then, toward the end of 1996, problems started showing up. Revenues started dropping—precipitously. Digital content distribution (video streaming) had appeared in the market, and customers were staying at home to stream movies into their living rooms—via cable, satellite, and, later, Netflix. Between 1996 and 2013, Blockbuster's board brought in two different CEOs to stop the bleeding and turn the company around. Each CEO believed that turning the stores into retailers would reinvigorate sales. At different times over the course of those seventeen years, Blockbuster began selling music, books, magazines, candy, popcorn, toys, apparel, and other goods. But, customers weren't buying any of it. In 2013, Blockbuster filed for bankruptcy.

The landscape is strewn with enterprises that did not adapt to environmental changes, disruptive innovations, or life cycle inevitabilities. The average lifespan of a company listed in the S&P 500 index of leading U.S. companies has decreased by more than fifty years in the last century, from sixty-seven years in the 1920s to just fifteen years today. On average, an S&P 500 company is now being replaced every two weeks.

Many factors have played a role in the downturn or demise of these enterprises. But, not adapting has one unique characteristic, and that is the subject of this chapter. Adapting or not adapting is fundamentally a human nature issue. Leaders come up with all kinds of explanations for not adapting, but, at the end of the day, it is who they are as people that they need to pay primary attention to. It is human nature to have difficulty with change when the demand for it comes from somewhere else. People can readily get on board with change that connects with their own (collectively decided upon) evolution and growth. But they do not like change that is forced upon them. When they have to deal with forced change, they, understandably, resist it.

Kodak was humming along until digital photography came along. Blockbuster was growing by leaps and bounds until video streaming showed up. They (like many companies when this happens) responded by sticking their heads in the sand, denying, trying quick fixes (e.g., selling candy and toys in a store that rents movies), changing the subject, believing that things were what they wanted them to be, refusing to face facts, etc..

Adaptation is important because you *will* be required to do it in order for your enterprise to succeed. Adaptations will be forced upon you. Many will be small, but if you don't make them, they will grow in severity. They need to be treated as opportunities, not something to avoid. Events that require adaptation are simply negative feedback. When the need for them arises, it means that something is not working. Andy Grove, the former CEO of Intel, once said: "The ability to recognize that the winds have shifted and to take appropriate action before you wreck your boat is crucial to the future of an enterprise."

Adaptation is very much like tacking a sailboat. Tacking literally means to change course by *turning a boat's head into and through the wind*. The mistake is to downplay the possible severity of the wind or try to get around it.

Lack of adaptation to what *your customer* is telling you is, probably, the biggest reason that bringing in a new CEO to "fix" an enterprise that's in trouble often does not work out. What boards too often don't do is to find out what customers are telling them before they choose a "fixer." How do you know whom to hire as your next CEO until you know why customers have stopped buying? Your customers have stopped buying for a reason. What is that reason? What can you do about it?

When business was starting to turn down, Blockbuster's board brought in a high-level executive from Walmart as the new CEO. The board did not know what the problem was, but that didn't stop the members from making this decision. Walmart is a retailer—Walmart sells a plethora of different kinds of goods. Blockbuster was a video-renting business (an entertainment business, if you will), not a retailer. The new CEO did not ask customers or existing executives any questions. He sidelined the executives and brought in his own executive team. His solution was to turn Blockbuster into a retailer—sell videos, not just rent them; sell popcorn, sodas, T-shirts, toys, candy, jeans, and other goods. It is not hard to understand why he did that—if the board chose to hire a retailer, then it was safe for the new CEO to assume that the board wanted a retailer. It did not work. In fact, customers not only didn't buy popcorn, sodas, etc.—they stopped renting videos.

Eight months later, the new CEO left the company. The board hired another retailer. He never asked customers or existing executives any questions, either. His solution was to turn Blockbuster into "another 7-Eleven." Eighteen months later, Blockbuster had lost all of its stock value and filed for bankruptcy.

Leading an enterprise is not about what *you* want your customers to pay for. It is about what your customers will pay for. Customers do not flock to your store because they want to help you keep your stock price up. They come to buy what they want. Blockbuster's leaders did not adapt to their customers—they didn't even ask them why they had stopped buying. They tried to get their customers to *adapt to them and what they wanted.*

Adaptation reconnects customers, employees, and leaders. Refusing to adapt breaks those connections. Ignoring or discounting what your customer is telling you is never a good idea. You may not like what your customer is telling you. The issue is not what you like or want. It is what your customers want. Kodak's and Blockbuster's customers were saying: We have found something better than what you are offering to us. But the companies didn't adapt, so customers walked away and eventually put both companies out of business.

If you want your enterprise to make money, adapt and deliver on your promise to your customers. If you want your enterprise to lose money, refuse to adapt and try to manipulate and exploit your customers.

The need to adapt is directly related to your customer promise. When your customer wind starts blowing and slowing you down or taking you entirely off course, you need to head directly into that wind and find out why they have stopped buying. Before Blockbuster's board did anything, it should have asked customers why they had stopped buying.

Kodak's and Blockbuster's demise has been consistently attributed to ineffective strategizing. The deeper reason is that both company's leaders were wedded to what they wanted. What they wanted for themselves trumped objective strategizing. Lack of adaption is rooted in human nature. That's why it is so important. Leaders infuse who they are as people into their reasoning process. But, most leaders don't give the importance of who they are as people its proper due. They typically don't ask: Is our decision really objective strategizing or is it just what I want or don't want? Leaders at Kodak and Blockbuster believed that things were what they wanted them to be. Lack of adaptation is fundamentally a *people-based* issue. In the world of free enterprise, new competitors appear on the scene, new technologies appear, slowdowns in economies occur. The demand to adapt goes with the territory. To ignore, deny, or discount new environmental changes that impact your kind of enterprise is, on its face, self-defeating. The only reason that leaders actually do that is their own personal subjectivity and what they want things to be. Objectively, there is no other explanation.

Your business will inevitably level off and hit a plateau. Complacency easily sets in—another natural human tendency. Adaptive enterprises understand this, and, when the time is right, they initiate activities to keep their enterprises growing. Adaptation is about building and continuing your prosperity. It's about lasting, continuing to grow, and staying connected with your customers.

Between 1939 and 1942, one of America's leading universities recruited 268 of its healthiest and most promising undergraduates to participate in a revolutionary new study of the human life cycle. The originators of the study wanted to learn the ways in which a group of promising individuals coped with their lives over the course of many years. Nearly forty years later, George Vaillant, director of the study, took the measure of the men. What he learned was that the men who coped best with the stresses in their lives were adaptive. He found that people's circumstances in life played no role in their eventual success or failure. What did differentiate those who succeeded from those who didn't was the ways that they coped with stress and adapted. The "adaptive" group got back up from the canvas, treated problems as opportunities, and dealt with obstacles head-on. They "headed directly into the wind." The same principle applies to profit and nonprofit living enterprises.

Signs That You Are Not Adapting

Newspaper advertising revenue from print has shrunk by nearly two-thirds since 2003, from $45 billion in 2003 to $16.4 billion in 2014. Between 1990 and 2010, 700 evening newspapers disappeared. The statistics all point down for newspapers. There are quite a few reasons. Direct marketing came along and said to local merchants: If your customers come from this limited geographical area, you don't need to advertise beyond this particular area, so why are you paying for advertising that covers a much wider area? Conglomerates came along, bought a spate of newspapers, went public and then demanded that those papers produce ever-improving financial returns, year in and year out. This drove publishers and their leadership teams to just focus on getting those returns, to the detriment of adaptation. Over time, it pushed editorial content more and more to areas that advertisers wanted (e.g., home improvement, gardens, etc.) and less and less to what readers were interested in. More and more editorial staff were let go, more in-depth reporting stopped, feature writing stopped, and the amount of space devoted to journalism got smaller and smaller. Monopolistic thinking grew and grew. This forced out weaker papers in local markets until one paper stood dominant. Then, the Internet came along. Given the dominance of advertising in newspapers, it was predictable that advertisers would move their ads to the Internet and leave newspapers because advertising on the Internet cost much less. As time went on, readers went away because, if they were interested in buying something, they could get the information that they needed from the Internet.

Newspapers have had a very tough time of it; they're under siege. Where they will end up is anybody's guess. However, if newspapers face the pressures head on and look at them as negative feedback and opportunities, they could fully adapt to what their customers are telling them that they need. Ignoring or discounting what customers are telling them will only make things worse. Basically, customers are telling newspapers that they prefer to get their news and information differently and that they want to pay less money. One adaptive option for local newspapers might be to change their core customer promise from predictable and dependable to customized. They could become "community information centers" that are tailored to their own local community(ies). They could become informational advocates for their local communities—garner needed information for them to solve problems and grow. They could utilize whatever medium (print, digital, etc.) that worked effectively for each unique community. That's one idea.

So, if your customers are leaving and your response is to ignore or discount that, you are not adapting. If your market research group comes to you and tells you that there is a new technology present in your marketplace that will replace your technology and that you have ten years to do something about it and you brush them off, you are not adapting. If your customers are walking away and your response is to try to come up with a way to manipulate them so that they will do what *you* want, you are not adapting.

The story of newspapers illustrates another natural human tendency that hinders adaptation. Threat raises fear and fear pushes leaders to monopolize. The strong and immediate tendency is to acquire competitors, to get bigger, and, thereby, increase one's power and sway in the marketplace. What we know about every human being's autonomic nervous system would predict this. Our autonomic nervous system is integrally linked to emotions. When threatened, we are all wired to fight or flight. Monopolizing is a way of fighting back. The bigger your army, the greater your chances of winning. In some spheres of endeavor, this may work. But, more often than not, it does not work. When it doesn't work, it usually has to do with inattention to what your customer is really telling you. If your fortunes are turning down and the major reason for that is that your customers are no longer interested in buying what you are selling, buying your competitors—whose customers are telling them the same thing—will only cause you to lose bigger. To this day, newspaper companies keep buying one another out. This approach is not working. Gaining more clout in the marketplace is not the solution. Customers have not stopped buying because newspapers aren't big enough. In many respects, monopolizing is actually emblematic of why customers are leaving. Customers are leaving because they don't want or need what you are selling. So, if you respond by gaining more size and clout to keep selling what they don't want, you are implicitly telling your customers to take it or leave it. They are already leaving it—monopolizing only reinforces their existing state of mind.

If you are inherently averse to conflict, then you are primed to not adapt and will not adapt when that conflict shows up. Conflict is negative feedback. You need to dig into conflict when it shows up, especially when the conflict is being generated by your customers, because the reason they are generating that conflict is crucial to your ability to adapt. If you aren't clear about the reason, then you have no idea about exactly what kind of adaptation you need to engage in. Conflict is simply bringing you information that you need to have. Looking into a conflict does not mean agreeing with the other parties; it does mean full consideration of what they are saying. If your enterprise motto is "don't make waves," you are not adapting.

If your customers are leaving and you spend most of your time on cost-cutting, you are not adapting. Cost control is important, but revenue (from delivering on your customer promise) is the deal. You can't save your way to prosperity—you need to adapt.

If you are letting stock price dictate your strategy, you are not adapting. If you ask your customers to sign a non-defamation contract and sue them if they say something negative about your customer service, you are not adapting. A pet care company in Texas did exactly this (sued a customer) when one of its customers posted a comment in Yelp that the company "overfed their fish." This company is not adapting. If you are not asking yourselves "where do we need to innovate?" on some kind of regular basis, that is a sign that you and your enterprise are prone toward lack of adaptation. If you think you can control what your customers say about you that is a sure sign that you should not go into your own business at all.

How to Ensure That Your Enterprise Continues to Adapt to Inevitable Changes in the Marketplace

Mercedes-Benz Credit Corporation (MBCC) finances Daimler-Benz products in North America. In 1992, it had its most profitable year in company history. For the first time, revenues topped $1 billion. In spite of this, CEO Georg Bauer was worried. He realized all too clearly that MBCC's competitive advantages would soon be wiped out by shifts in the market. In particular, Japanese makers of luxury cars were on the rise and would continue to offer attractive lease deals. Additionally, leasing and finance were becoming commodities. Soon, any bank could offer better rates than MBCC.

Bauer chose to interpret these approaching marketplace changes as opportunities. Rather than bemoan them, he embraced them and saw them as an exciting challenge. He knew the answer was for MBCC to change *itself*. Complacence was showing up in the company. Fiefdoms had emerged. Everyone was assuming that they would continue to be successful by doing what they had always done. He wondered if he should wait until the company was feeling the pain of losing competitive advantage or catalyze the needed changes right away. He chose the latter. He instinctively knew that people do not like (and resist) change that is imposed on them. So, he brought the whole company into the change effort. He did not rush in and restructure the company, which happens with alarming regularity in the business world. Instead of directly addressing MBCC's existing structure, he left it alone (for a later day) and worked around it.

He and his executive team met with everyone in the company and explained the competitive pressures the company would soon face. He told his employees that these coming pressures were opportunities and that he needed co-problem-solvers and co-developers to get the company ready to capitalize on the coming marketplace changes. He told everyone that they all needed to take the challenges ahead into their own hands and create a different future for the company. He emphasized that the central goal was to *competitively, profitably, and successfully deliver on its promise to its customers.* He gave an ear to everyone's concerns and questions. The company had to get on with it, so he established how the big decisions had to be made. They didn't have time to come to consensus on every issue. They did have time to get everyone's ideas and solutions. But, given the challenges coming, he needed to make the final decision if people could not agree. He said that, if his decision was wrong, he would get more ideas and, then, try another solution. He also created a company-wide and generous profit-sharing program that applied to everyone in the company. This program was based on company performance.

People signed on to the challenge. Bauer and his fellow leaders formed a project team, representing a cross-section of managers and employees. This team studied the company and the marketplace, elicited ideas from everyone in the company, and recommended nineteen initiatives. These initiatives were all accepted by Bauer and his fellow executives. The team built a set of goals and plans for accomplishing those goals, which senior leadership also agreed with. Plans included pilot tests for quite a few of the initiatives. As initiatives were implemented, Bauer and his employees celebrated accomplishments all along the way.

Five years later, MBCC was leading its market in both market share and customer/dealer satisfaction. When market changes materialized, the company was ready. Most of the nineteen initiatives were centered on learning from the company's customers and most of the changes made were based on feedback from customers. Customers were angered by the complexity of MBCC's lease agreement, so the company redesigned it to make it easier for customers to understand. The company offered a range of options regarding the time of leases instead of just offering the standard thirty-six-month lease. The company crafted lease agreements around what its *customers* believed were important, not what MBCC thought or wanted. This enhanced the value of financing for customers and it paid off significantly.

What Georg Bauer, his fellow leaders, and employees did serves as a model for adaptation and how to do it. Every enterprise's situation will be different and details will be different, but, in general, this MBCC example provides a picture of the fundamentals of adapting. They are:

- Keep working to get an ongoing picture of the future of your market.
- Anticipate market and competitor changes.
- When evidence indicates that your enterprise needs to make changes, communicate that to your whole enterprise. Describe the coming changes as challenges and opportunities.
- Get everyone's thinking, questions, ideas, and concerns about what is happening and capture where people agree and disagree. Create a process whereby everyone, not just leadership, resolves these disagreements. Let your and their logic be the essential source of resolution, not titles. If agreement cannot be reached and you are running out of time, make the decision and, then, track how it is working.
- Create the *conditions* necessary for collective judgment-making.
- Emphasize that the central goal is to competitively, profitably, and successfully deliver on your customer promise.
- Create a profit-sharing program so that everyone benefits if your enterprise succeeds.
- Build and implement a goal-attainment system.
- Celebrate accomplishments all along the way.

Lead your enterprise as a living people system. It works! You, your fellow leaders, your employees, and your customers are an interdependent living system. Your customers are not "outside" your enterprise. Staying profitably connected with your customers is a major key to your success. If your customers start disconnecting with you and your enterprise, pay very close attention and find out why they are doing that. When you get the answer, make the necessary adaptations. If you discount, neglect, or ignore your customers, you are doing the same thing to yourselves.

Vaillant's research results get to the heart of adaptation and why it is so important. In the bigger picture and over the longer term, your enterprise's continued success or failure hinges on your (human) response to the circumstances that the world of free enterprise brings to you, your fellow leaders, and your employees. You and your enterprise are in an interdependent network with your customers. When your customers push back or pull away, they are dis-ordering your relationship with them. Refusing to adapt with them is, actually, debilitating you and your enterprise. Adaptation strengthens you and your enterprise. At the end of the day, "heading directly into the wind" with your customer is the only real option that you have.

12

CONCLUSION

➤ ➤ ➤

Please look at the nine dots in Figure 12-1. Your task is to connect the nine dots by four straight lines without lifting the pencil from the paper. It will likely help if you try the solution on a piece of paper before reading on and especially before turning to the solution (Figure 12-2).

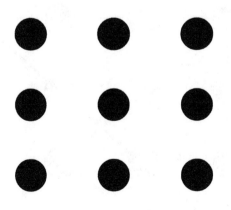

Figure 12-1. Nine Dots

Almost everybody who tries to solve this problem immediately adopts as part of his problem-solving approach an assumption that makes the solution impossible. The assumption is that the dots compose a square and that the solution must be found within that square, a self-imposed condition that the instructions do not contain. His failure, therefore, does not lie in the impossibility of the task, but in the assumption that he immediately makes and his attempted solution. Having now created the problem, it does not matter in the least which combination of four lines he now tries, and in what order; he always finishes with the square but will never solve the task. The solution entails a different kind of change, which consists in leaving the field—"thinking outside of the box (square)," if you will.

Immediately assuming that the nine dots compose a square and that the solution must be found within that square establishes a mindset that solidifies a certain way of thinking and pattern of action. As long as one stays convinced that the only way to solve the problem requires the preservation of this mind-set, the problem cannot be solved. The only way that it can be solved is to tackle the problem with a different mind-set. The problem solver has to step out of the set of nine dots and see if there is another way to follow the rules and accomplish the goal.

When the problem solver steps out of the system of nine dots, there is a solution that emerges. The solution to the nine-dot problem is portrayed in Figure 12-2.

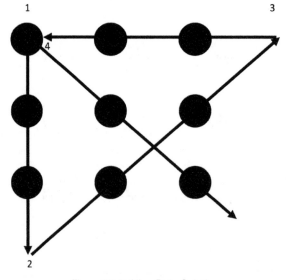

Figure 12-2. Nine Dots Solution

The nine-dot problem and its solution is an analogy for what this book is asking you to do. Operating from the assumption of individual-centricity is equivalent to assuming that the set of nine dots is a "square." Put another way, the individual-centric mind-set keeps us locked into addressing the problem from a "one dot (individual) at a time" paradigm. The nine-dot problem solution involves addressing the problem from a system-centric mind-set. But, you have to step out of the field (system) to do that. This book gives you a practical way to do that.

Adopting a system-centric mind-set; leading your enterprise as a living people system; properly connecting your customers, employees, and your fellow leaders; and ensuring that your particular customer promise determines how you lead and build your culture brings you a myriad of benefits:

- Shows you the root causes of your people problems and gives you a way to solve those problems—and keep them from reappearing
- Frees up your fellow leaders and employees, releases positive energy, and creates the conditions for spontaneous (self-generating) development—creates a virtuous cycle
- Ties everything to the delivery of your customer promise
- Unifies your enterprise

I hope that this book makes a substantive and lasting contribution to your, your fellow leaders', your employees' and your customers' success.

APPENDIX ANALYTICS

Using the Validated Assessments Available to You and Your Enterprise

The analytics described here have all been scientifically validated. The validation process took more than six years. The database (size of sample) for this validation work comprises more than 33,800 people.

At the time of this writing, these assessments have been utilized in some fifty-seven enterprises. Via our work with our own clients and the clients of our 260 network consultants, more than 18,000 leaders have completed one or more of these assessments.

The major benefits of these assessments are:

- Objective measure of your enterprise's core customer promise, core and support unit cultures, and core and support unit leadership approaches
- Objective measure of the extent to which your enterprise overall and each unit are focused
- Objective measure of the extent to which your enterprise's customer promise, culture, and leadership are integrated (properly connected)—including all fifteen cultural drivers and the three leadership drivers
- Objective measure of the extent to which your leaders and employees agree with one another regarding customer promise, culture, leadership, and the extent to which your enterprise is integrated
- Results provide verifiable data for developing an actionable roadmap for more effectively delivering on your customer promise
- Objective measure of your individual approach to leadership, fit with core customer promise, and core culture

- Objective measure of an individual contributor's approach to work and fit with your enterprise's culture

The Enterprise-Level Assessments

The three enterprise-level assessments (ECPI, ECI, ELTI) provide the most benefit when administered together. There are times when one or more of them would, advisedly, be administered separately, but, measuring the *nature and degree of connection* between customer promise, culture, and leadership is where the major payoff lies.

Enterprise Customer Promise Indicator (ECPI)™

The ECPI measures how leaders and employees perceive the core customer promise of their enterprise and of each unit. It measures the extent to which people are in agreement with one another. It simply asks each respondent to indicate whether or not his or her enterprise promises a particular offering or outcome. For example, a respondent is asked if his or her enterprise promises: 1. Excellent, highly superior product or service; 2. High degree of production capacity and capability; 3. Highly customized product or service; or 4. A fuller, better life.

This assessment is focused on the enterprise as a whole and/or its units (departments, team, etc.). It is administered to a stratified sample of leaders, managers, and employees. The results of the assessment can be cut any way desired by the enterprise—by tenure, position, age, unit, geographical area, function, etc.

It was validated several ways. One, we asked independent consultants who were familiar with our framework to go into separate enterprises within which we had administered the ECPI and interview a stratified sample of leaders and employees. They independently determined the core customer promises for each of these enterprises, and we then determined the degree of correlations between the results of the ECPI and the consultant interviews. We also predicted that certain kinds of enterprises would result in one of the four customer promises and, then, administered the ECPI to those types of enterprises. We then determined the extent to which our predictions came true—based on the results of the ECPI.

Enterprise Culture Indicator (ECI)™

The ECI measures core culture and fifteen culture drivers. It measures the enterprise as a whole and/or its units. It is administered to a stratified sample of leaders, managers, and employees. The results of the assessment can be cut any way desired by the enterprise—by tenure, position, age, unit, geographical area, function, etc.

This assessment is a prevalence measure. It is entirely composed of behavioral items and the extent to which these behaviors are experienced (prevalence of behaviors) by those completing the assessment. Items are not right or wrong, bad or good. They simply ask respondents what is actually occurring in their whole enterprise and/or unit. All of the choices are actual behaviors. For example, one item asks: "The structure of our enterprise is: 1. Whatever works to get our ideals accomplished; 2. Groups or clusters of people with their customers; 3. Levels of authority and required functions; 4. Managers and experts on project teams." Respondents rate each choice for "Not True" to "Very Much True."

Validation work includes factor analysis, concept validity studies, and reliability studies. Actual validation work mirrors the approaches mentioned regarding the ECPI.

Enterprise Leadership Team Indicator (ELTI)™

The Individual-Level Assessments

Individual Leader Indicator (ILI)™

This assessment provides an individual leader with a picture of his or her central approach to leadership. It also tells the leader which customer promise and culture are most consistent with his or her approach. It describes his or her strengths and potential pitfalls as a leader. It also shows how to adapt his or her leadership behavior to an enterprise that is less suited to his/her natural approach.

It is a twenty-item self-rated questionnaire that asks the respondent to determine what is "most true" and "next most true" about him or her. All of the choices are positive choices. Items cover behavior, values, motives, beliefs, self-concept, and traits.

It was validated by way of factor analysis, construct validity studies, and reliability studies. We also studied type of leadership approach and its predicted fit with each of the four core cultures.

Individual Contributor Indicator (ICI)™

This assessment measures an individual contributor's central personal characteristics and fit with enterprise culture. It provides information on: basic work approach, motivations, values, and personal style. It also measures fit with culture. It entails the use of a questionnaire similar to the ILI and was validated the same way as the ILI.

REFERENCES

Abrashoff, D. M. *It's Your Ship: Management Techniques from the Best Damn Ship in the Navy.* New York: Grand Central Publishing, Updated Edition, 2012.

Aceto, P. *Weology: How Everybody Wins When We Comes Before Me.* New York: HarperCollins Publishers, 2015.

Ahamed, L. *Lords of Finance: The Bankers Who Broke the World.* New York: Penguin, 2009.

Alexander, L. "Obama May Have Overcorrected on the Overtesting Problem." *Time,* November 9, 2015.

Allaccess staff. "Cumulus Q3 Revenue Down 7.8%, EBITDA Off 11.5%." Allaccess .com, November 5, 2015.

Amabile, T., Fisher, C. M., and Pillemer, J. "IDEO's Culture of Helping: By Making Collaborative Generosity the Norm, the Design Firm Has Unleashed Its Creativity." *Harvard Business Review,* January–February 2014, 55–61.

Anderson, C. "The 'New' Performance Management—What We Were Supposed to Be Doing All Along?" Bizcatalyst.com, December 13, 2015.

Arango, T. "How the AOL-Time Warner Merger Went So Wrong." *New York Times,* January 10, 2010.

Armstrong, M. "Mainstream vs. Austrian Economics." Armstrong Economics blog, November 6, 2015.

Aspan, M. "The $520 Million Company That's Solving All Your Financial Needs." Inc.com, February 2016.

Aulet, B. "Culture Eats Strategy for Breakfast." TechCrunch.com, April 12, 2014.

Barankay, I. "Why It's Sometimes Better Not to Tell Employees Where They Stand." Knowledge@Wharton, September 4, 2015.

Barlow, Z., and Stone, M. K. "Living Systems and Leadership: Cultivating Conditions for Institutional Change." *Journal of Sustainability Education,* vol. 2, March 2011.

Barnard, C. *The Functions of the Executive.* Cambridge, MA: Harvard University Press, 1938.

Barney, J. B. "Organizational Culture: Can It Be a Source of Sustained Competitive Advantage?" *Academy of Management Review,* vol. 11 (July 1986), 656–665.

Barr, A. "Zappos CEO Distances Shoe Retailer's Culture from Amazon." *Wall Street Journal,* October 20, 2015.

Baskin, K. *Corporate DNA: Learning from Life*. Boston: Butterworth Heinemann, 1998.

Bateson, G. *Steps to an Ecology of Mind: Collected Essays in Anthropology, Psychiatry, Evolution, and Epistemology*. Chicago: University of Chicago Press, 1972.

Bernstein, E., Bunch, J., Canner, N., and Lee, M. "Beyond the Holacracy Hype: The Overwrought Claims—and Actual Promise—of the Next Generation of Self-Managed Teams." *Harvard Business Review*, July-August 2016.

Bershidsky, L. "Today's Tech Is like Yesterday's Wall Street." *Denver Post*, August 21, 2015.

Bhalla, V. "How to Stop Wasting $40 Billion on Leadership and Talent." *Economic Times*, July 24, 2015.

Biro, M. M. "You're Hired and It's Mutual: 5 Ways Employee Culture Is Great for Leaders." *Forbes*, November 30, 2014.

Bishop, T. "15,000 Robots and Counting: Inside Amazon's New Fulfillment Centers." Geekwire, November 30, 2014.

Bookbinder, D. "The New ROI: Return on Individuals—Chapter 1: The Value of the Workforce." Huffington Post, March 9, 2016.

Boudreau, J., and Rice, S. "Bright, Shiny Objects and the Future of HR." *Harvard Business Review*, July–August 2015.

Bruch, H., and Vogel, B. *Fully Charged: How Great Leaders Boost Their Organization's Energy and Ignite High Performance*. Boston: Harvard Business Press, 2011.

Bryant, A. "Joshua Reeves of Gusto: Directing Without Dictating." *Business Day, New York Times*, March 4, 2016.

Burton, T. T., and Moran, J. W. *The Future Focused Organization: Complete Organizational Alignment for Breakthrough Results*. Englewood Cliffs, NJ: Prentice-Hall, 1995.

Byrnes, B. "Costco Co-Founder: 'Culture Is Not the Most Important Thing—It's the Only Thing.'" Motley Fool [fool.com], August 21, 2013.

Cappelli, P. "Why We Love to Hate HR . . . and What HR Can Do About It." *Harvard Business Review*, July–August 2015.

Capra, F. *The Hidden Connections: A Science for Sustainable Living*. New York: Anchor Books, 2002.

Capra, F. *The Web of Life: A New Scientific Understanding of Living Systems*. New York: Anchor Books, 1996.

Carey, K. "Corinthian Colleges Is Closing. Its Students May be Better Off as a Result." *The Upshot, New York Times*, July 2, 2014.

Chandler, G. "Tech Supplier CEO Shares 'Truly Human Leadership' Philosophy with Lakeshore Business Leaders." *Grand Rapids Press*, September 3, 2014.

Charan, R., Barton, D., and Carey, D. "People Before Strategy: A New Role for the CHRO." *Harvard Business Review*, July–August 2015.

Christensen, C. M., and Shu, K. "What Is an Organization's Culture?" Harvard Business School Note 399–104, 2006.

Christensen, C. M., and van Bever, D. "The Capitalist's Dilemma: The Tools We Use to Guide Our Investments Are Blind to the Best Opportunities for Creating New Jobs and New Markets." *Harvard Business Review*, 2014, 61–68.

Coffman, C. W., and Sorensen, K. *Culture Eats Strategy for Lunch: The Secret of Extraordinary Results, Igniting the Passion Within.* Denver: Liang Addison Press, 2013.

Cohen, R. "Capitalism Eating Its Children." *New York Times, The Opinion Pages,* May 29, 2014.

Collins, J. C., and Porras, J. I. *Built to Last: Successful Habits of Visionary Companies.* New York: HarperCollins Publishers, 1994.

Colvin, G. "How to Build the Perfect Workplace." *Fortune,* March 5, 2015.

Conger, J. A., & Associates. *Spirit at Work.* San Francisco: Jossey-Bass Publishers, 1994.

Covey, S. R. *Principle-Centered Leadership.* New York: Fireside, 1992.

Covey, S. R. *The Seven Habits of Highly Effective People.* New York: Simon & Schuster, 1989.

Coyne, T. "10 Steps to Improve Student Learning." *Denver Post,* November 20, 2015.

Cross, R., Rebele, R., and Grant, A. "Collaborative Overload." *Harvard Business Review,* January–February 2016.

Cunningham, L., "Tony Hsieh Got Rid of Bosses at Zappos, and That's Not Even His Biggest Idea." *Washington Post,* December 1, 2015.

Cunningham, L., and McGregor, J. "Performance Reviews Are Falling out of Favor." *Denver Post,* August 23, 2015.

Daley, M. "Lawmaker: Michigan Governor Responsible for Flint Crisis." Associated Press, March 17, 2016.

De Geus, A. *The Living Company: Habits for Survival in a Turbulent Business Environment.* Boston: Harvard Business School Press, 1997.

Denninger, K. "The Destruction of an American Brand." Market Ticker (market-ticker.org), April 7, 2014.

DePree, M. *Leadership Is an Art.* New York: Dell Publishing, 1989.

DesMarais, C. "Why Your Employees Should Come Before Customers." *Inc* magazine (inc.com), November 18, 2014.

Dobbs, R., Leslie, K., and Mendonca, L. T. "Building the Healthy Corporation." *McKinsey Quarterly,* August 2005.

Donnithorne, L. R. *The West Point Way of Leadership.* New York: Currency Doubleday, 1993.

Drucker, P. F. *The Daily Drucker: 366 Days of Insight and Motivation for Getting the Right Things Done.* New York: HarperBusiness, 2004.

Dvorak, J. C. "The Slow, Sad Death of Yahoo." *Entrepreneur,* April 20, 2016.

Dweck, C. S. *Mindset: The New Psychology of Success. How We Can Learn to Fulfill Our Potential.* New York: Ballantine Books, 2006.

Edwards, H. S. "Leaving Tests Behind: The Backlash Against Standardized Tests Has Left Lawmakers Searching for Ways to Keep Parents Happy yet Still Hold Schools, and Students, Accountable." *Time,* February 16, 2015.

Eggers, D. *The Circle.* New York: Vintage Books, 2014.

Ehrenkrantz, D. "Why You Should Run Your Business like a Nonprofit." *Forbes,* February 26, 2014.

Eichenwald, K. "How Microsoft Lost Its Mojo: Steve Ballmer and Corporate America's Most Spectacular Decline." *Vanity Fair,* August 1, 2012.

Evans, L. "This Is How Millennials Will Change Management." FastCompany .com, October 29, 2015.

Everingham, J. "The Principles of Quantum Team Management." Firstround.com, June 10, 2016.

Fallon, N. "Your Employees Don't All Want the Same Company Culture . . . Now What?" *Business News Daily*, October 8, 2014.

Fallows, J. "How America Is Putting Itself Back Together." *Atlantic*, March 2016.

Ferro, S. "The Story Behind the Craziest Corporate Collapse of the Last Decade." Huffington Post, March 23, 2016.

Fiegerman, S. "How Yahoo Derailed Tumblr: After Marissa Mayer Promised 'Not to Screw It Up.'" Mashable, June 15, 2016.

Fischer, B. "Three Cheers for the End of Google as We Knew It." *Forbes*, August 11, 2015.

Fluermach. "Einstein on Interdependence." Fleurmach.com. September 21, 2012.

Foroohar, R. "How Clintonomics Created Carly Fiorina—and Hampers Hillary." *Time*, October 26, 2015.

Foroohar, R. "Saving Capitalism." *Time*, May 12, 2016.

Foroohar, R. "Wall Street's Values Are Strangling American Business." *Time*, July 10, 2014.

Fortune Editors. "The Results of the 2015 Fortune 500 CEO Survey Are In." *Fortune*, June 4, 2015.

Fry, E. "Nestle's Half-Billion-Dollar Noodle Debacle in India." *Fortune*, April 26, 2016.

Gagnon, B. "Why Strategies Get Stuck." Fcw.com, February 17, 2015.

Gallup, Inc. "State of the American Workplace Report," 2013.

Gerstner, L. "Lou Gerstner on Corporate Reinvention and Values." *McKinsey Quarterly*, September 2014.

Gillett, R. "Infographic: How Much a Bad Hire Will Actually Cost You." Fast Company, April 8, 2014.

Gitelson, G., Bing, J. W., and Laroche, L. "The Impact of Culture on Mergers and Acquisitions." CMA Management. March 2001.

Goldratt, E. "The Goal." Great Barrington, MA: North River Press. 1992 (2nd Revised Edition).

Goll, I., and Sambharya, R. B. "Corporate Ideology, Diversification and Firm Performance." *Organization Studies*, vol. 15, no. 5 (Winter 1995), 823–847.

Graber, M. "Regenerate Corporate Cultures." *Memphis Daily News*, September 8, 2014.

Graffin, G. "'Survival of the Fittest' Is a Sham." *Time*, September 10, 2015.

Griffith, E. "Fixing Twitter." *Fortune*, March 8, 2016.

Grove, A. S. *High Output Management*. New York: Vintage Books, 1995.

Hagel, J., and Singer, M. "Unbundling the Corporation." *Harvard Business Review*, March–April 1999.

Hammonds, K. H. "Why We Hate HR." Fast Company, August 1, 2005.

Handy, C. *The Hungry Spirit: Beyond Capitalism: A Quest for Purpose in the Modern World*. New York: Broadway Books, 1998.

Hansen, J. L., with Christensen, P.A. *Invisible Patterns: Ecology and Wisdom in Business and Profit*. Westport, CT: Quorum Books, 1995.

Heimans, J. "Uber's New Power Failure: Uber Built a Model Network, But Failed to Match That Excellence in Values." Fast Company, November 26, 2014.

Heskett, J. L. *The Culture Cycle: How to Shape the Unseen Force That Transforms Performance.* Upper Saddle River, NJ: FT Press, 2012.

Hesselbein, F., Goldsmith, M., and Beckhard, R. *The Organization of the Future.* San Francisco: Jossey-Bass Publishers, 1997.

Holland, J. H. *Emergence: From Chaos to Order.* Reading, MA: Helix Books, 1998.

Holliday, M. "What You See Is What You Get: The Full Promise of Seeing Your Organization as a Living System." Huffington Post Business Blog, April 27, 2015.

Huy, Q., and Vuori, T. "Who Killed Nokia? Nokia Did." Knowledge.INSEAD. September 22, 2015.

Ingram, M. "Dysfunctional Train Wreck at Tribune Publishing Rolls On." Fortune .com, October 15, 2015.

Isidore, C. "GM's Total Recall Cost: $4.1 billion." CNNMoney, February 4, 2015.

Janofsky, A. "Marcus Lemonis: How to Grow Your Company by Splitting It in Two." *Inc. Magazine* (online), December 29, 2015.

Johnson, S. "The Quiet Coup." *Atlantic,* May 2009.

Keidel, R. W. *Seeing Organizational Patterns.* San Francisco: Berrett-Koehler Publishers, 1995.

Kirp, D. L. "Teaching Is Not a Business." *New York Times, The Opinion Pages,* August 17, 2014.

Kotter, J. P., and Heskett, J. L. *Corporate Culture and Performance.* New York: The Free Press, 1992.

Lapavitsas, C. *Profiting Without Producing: How Finance Exploits Us All.* New York: Verso Books, 2014.

Lazonick, W. "Profits Without Prosperity." *Harvard Business Review,* September 2014.

LeClaire, J. "Microsoft Shakes Up Senior Leadership Team." Top Tech News, June 22, 2015.

Lender, J. "Times Are Tough at Water Agency—But CEO Still Gets Big Raise, Sweet Pension Deal." *Hartford Courant,* March 5, 2016.

Lipman, V. "Surprising, Disturbing Facts from the Mother of All Employee Engagement Surveys." Forbes.com. September 23, 2013.

Lorsch, J. W. "Culture Is Not the Culprit: When Organizations Are in Crisis, It's Usually Because the Business Is Broken." *Harvard Business Review,* April 2016.

Lorsch, J. W. "Managing Culture: The Invisible Barrier to Strategic Change." *California Management Review,* vol. 28, no. 2 (Winter 1986), 95–109.

Lucier, C. "Herb Kelleher: The Thought Leader Interview: The Co-founder and Chairman of Southwest Airlines Tells Why a Firm's People Are Everything." *Strategy+Business,* June 1, 2004.

Maira, A., and Scott-Morgan, P. *The Accelerating Organization: Embracing the Human Face of Change.* New York: McGraw-Hill, 1997.

Marcus, R. "Costly Quest to Fix Failing Schools." *Quad-City Times,* October 20, 2015.

Margulis, L. "Gaia, the Living Earth: A Dialogue with Fritjof Capra." *Elmwood Newsletter,* Berkeley, CA, vol. 5, no. 2, 1989.

Margulis, L., and Sagan, D. *Microcosmos: Four Billion Years of Evolution from Our Microbial Ancestors.* London: Allen & Unwin, 1987.

Markkula Center for Applied Ethics (Santa Clara University). "Lessons from the Enron Scandal." Interview with Kirk Hanson. March 5, 2002.

Martin, J. "The False Premise of the Shareholder Value Debate." *Harvard Business Review*, September 26, 2016.

Martin, J. "For Senior Leaders, Fit Matters More than Skill." *Harvard Business Review*, January 17, 2014.

Maturana, H., and Varela, F. *The Tree of Knowledge.* Boston: Shambhala, 1987.

Mauldin, J. "The Financialization of the Economy." MauldinEconomics.com, October 28, 2015.

McChrystal, S., Collins, T., Silverman, D., and Fussell, C. "Let General Stanley McChrystal Explain Why Adaptability Trumps Hierarchy." Fast Company, May 12, 2015.

McGregor, J. "Zappos Says 18 Percent of Company Has Left Following Its Radical 'No Bosses' Approach." *Washington Post*, January 14, 2016.

Micklethwait, J., and Wooldridge, A. *The Witch Doctors: Making Sense of the Management Gurus.* New York: Times Books, 1996.

Mintzberg, H., Ahlstrand, B., and Lampel, J. "Management? It's Not What You Think!" New York: AMACOM, 2010.

Mochari, I. "Workplace Monitoring Can Hinder Productivity." *Denver Post*, April 3, 2016.

Montier, J. "The World's Dumbest Idea." GMO White Paper at gmo.com, December 2014.

Morris, T. "Crafting a Customer Centric Culture: 3 Key Factors." Parature, December 11, 2013.

Mui, C. "How Kodak Failed." Forbes.com, January 18, 2012.

Mui, C., and Carroll, P. *Billion Dollar Lessons: What You Can Learn From the Most Inexcusable Business Failures of the Last 25 Years.* New York: Portfolio, 2009.

Mukunda, G. "The Price of Wall Street's Power: How the Financial Sector's Outsize Influence Is Undermining Business." *Harvard Business Review*, June 2014, 71–78.

Mulgan, G. *Connexity.* London: Vintage, 1998.

Mycoskie, B. "The Founder of TOMS on Reimagining the Company's Mission." *Harvard Business Review*, January–February 2016.

Neilson, G. L., Estupinan, J., and Sethi, B. "10 Principles of Organizational Design." Strategy+Business, March 23, 2015.

Nichols, J., and McChesney, R. W. *Dollarocracy: How the Money and Media Election Complex Is Destroying America.* New York: Nation Books, 2014.

Nirenberg, J. *The Living Organization: Transforming Teams into Workplace Communities.* Burr Ridge, IL: Irwin Professional Publishing. 1993.

Norton, D., Helland, S., Nye, G., and McClaren, J. "Promises, Promises: Easily Made, Easily Broken. What Companies Are Saying Versus Actually Doing—and How Customers Are Responding." Accenture, 2014.

Nusca, A. "Microsoft Will Serve You Now." *Fortune*, June 9, 2016.

Oakley, E., and Krug, D. "*Enlightened Leadership.* New York: Simon & Schuster, 1991.

O'Connor, M., and Dornfeld, B. *The Moment You Can't Ignore: When Big Trouble Leads to a Great Future.* New York: Public Affairs, 2014.

O'Connor, R. J. "From the Archive, 1996: The End of Apple's Crusade." *San Jose Mercury News.* August 29, 2014 (originally appeared January 28, 1996).

O'Connor-Cahill, M. E. "Person-Culture Fit: A Study of How the Congruence Between Person and Culture Relates to Employee Perceptions of Organizational Fit, Job Satisfaction, Organizational Commitment, and Intent to Leave." Los Angeles: UMI, 2001.

Ogden, C. "Networks and Living Systems Patterns." Interaction Institute for Social Change, November 20, 2013.

Olson, M. S., van Bever, D., and Verry, S. "When Growth Stalls," *Harvard Business Review,* March 2008.

Peters, T. J., and Waterman, R. H., Jr. *In Search of Excellence: Lessons from America's Best-Run Companies."* New York: Harper & Row Publishers, Inc. 1982.

Peterson, H., "Sears' Obsession with Wall Street Is Killing the Retailer for Good." Business Insider, June 16, 2016.

Pontefract, D. *Flat Army: Creating a Connected and Engaged Organization.* New York: Wiley, 2013.

Prigogine, I. *From Being to Becoming.* San Francisco: Freeman, 1980.

Putman, A. O. "Organizations." In A. O. Putman and K. E. Davis (Eds.), *Advances in Descriptive Psychology.* Ann Arbor, MI: Descriptive Psychology Press, 1990, vol. 5, 11–46.

Randall, L. *Dark Matter and the Dinosaurs: The Astounding Interconnectedness of the Universe.* New York: Ecco Press, 2015.

Rao, S. R. "Taking Charge of Corporate Culture." Citeman Network (citeman.com), November 10, 2008.

Reeves, M., Haanaes, K., and Sinha, J. *Your Strategy Needs a Strategy: How to Choose and Execute the Right Approach.* Boston: Harvard Business Review Press, 2015.

Reingold, J., "How a Radical Shift Left Zappos Reeling." *Fortune,* March 4, 2016.

Reingold, J., "Southwest's Herb Kelleher: Still Crazy After All These Years." *Fortune,* January 14, 2013.

Robert, M. *Strategy: Pure and Simple.* New York: McGraw-Hill, 1993.

Robertson, A., and Leumer, B. "Towards the Privatization of Public Education in America. Imposing a Corporate Culture." Montreal, Canada: Centre for Research on Globalization. January 11, 2014.

Robles, Y. "Evolution of Teacher Evaluations Is Leading Performance Pay Reforms" *Denver Post,* July 27, 2015.

Roden, S. "The Moral Dimensions of Business." *Huffington Post,* June 12, 2015.

Rogers, R. W., Hayden, J. W., and Ferketish, B. J. *Organizational Change That Works.* Pittsburgh, PA: DDI Press, 1997.

Roll, M. "Culture Can Make or Break Strategy." INSEAD Knowledge, December 3, 2014.

Roushar, J. "Modeling Positive and Negative Activation." UnderstandingContext.com, August 18, 2014.

Ryan, L. "PayPal President to Staff: Use Our Stuff, or Take a Hike." Huffington Post, February 12, 2014.

Sandel, M. "What Isn't for Sale?" *The Atlantic*, April 2012.

Sandel, M. *What Money Can't Buy: The Moral Limits of Markets*. New York: Farrar, Straus and Giroux, Reprint ed., 2013.

Satell, G. "Culture Can Be a Trap—Here's How to Make It an Asset." *Forbes Tech*, July 18, 2015.

Schippmann, J. S. *Strategic Job Modeling: Working at the Core of Integrated Human Resources*. Mahwah, NJ: Lawrence Erlbaum Associates, 1999.

Schneider, A. "Using Big Data to Better Connect with People." Huffington Post, April 14, 2016.

Schneider, W. E. "Aligning Strategy, Culture and Leadership." In J. E. Neumann, K. Kellner, and A. Dawson-Shepherd (Eds.), Developing *Organisational Consultancy*. London: Routledge, 1997, 250–266.

Schneider, W. E. "Culturelink." Copyright 2003–2014. Individual Contributor Reports (4).

Schneider, W. E. "Culturetek: Linking Strategy and Leadership to Bottom Line Performance." Copyright 2000/2014. Training Program.

Schneider, W. E. "The 5 Things Effective Leaders Do." *MWorld*, Fall 2003, 20–23.

Schneider, W. E. *"Leadership Culturelink."* Copyright 2003–2014. Individual Leadership Reports (4).

Schneider, W. E. "The Paradigm Shift in Human Resources." *Personnel Journal*, November 1985, 14–16.

Schneider, W. E. "Productivity Improvement Through Cultural Focus." *Consulting Psychology Journal: Practice and Research*, vol. 47, no. 1 (Winter 1995), 3–27.

Schneider, W. E. "Results-Oriented Leadership Vital to Managing Changes." *Utility Executive*, vol. 3, no. 6 (November-December 2000).

Schneider, W. E., "Trouble at the Top: A Sign of Deal Disorder." *Mergers and Acquisitions: The Dealmaker's Journal*, vol. 38, no. 4 (April 2003), 30–32.

Schneider, W. E. "Why Good Management Ideas Fail." *Focus on Change Management*, 44–45, May-June 1998.

Schneider, W. E. "Why Strategies Fall Apart: The CEO/Culture Disconnect." *2003 Handbook of Business Strategy*, vol. 4, no. 1 (2003), 174–180.

Schwartz, H., and Davis, S. "Matching Corporate Culture and Business Strategy." *Organizational Dynamics*, 10 (Summer 1981), 30–48.

Scott, B. "Reid Hoffman: A.I. Is Going to Change Everything About Managing Teams." Inc., July 7, 2016.

Senge, P. *The Fifth Discipline: The Art and Practice of the Learning Organization*. New York: Doubleday, 1990.

Senn, L. "Cultural Transformation Only Comes with Personal Transformation." CultureUniversity.com, 2014.

Sheridan, K. *Building a Magnetic Culture: How to Attract and Retain Top Talent to Create an Engaged, Productive Workforce*. New York: McGraw-Hill, 2012.

Sheridan, R. *Joy, Inc.: How We Built a Workplace People Love*. New York: Portfolio/Penguin, 2013.

Sherman, E. "Sears CEO Eddie Lampert Should Stop Reading Ayn Rand." Inc.com, August 17, 2015.

Shrivastava, P. "Integrating Strategy Formulation with Organizational Culture." *Journal of Business Strategy*, vol. 5, no. 3 (1985), 103–111.

Sibbet, D., and the Staff of HBR. "75 Years of Management Ideas and Practice 1922–1997: A Supplement to the *Harvard Business Review.*" *Harvard Business Review*, September–October 1997.

Sisodia, R. S., Sheth, J. N., and Wolfe, D. B. *Firms of Endearment: How World-Class Companies Profit from Passion and Purpose.* Upper Saddle River, NJ: Pearson FT Press, 2014.

Smith, G., "Why I Am Leaving Goldman Sachs." *New York Times*, March 14, 2012.

Snipes, P. "My Years at Wal-Mart." CounterPunch, December 3, 2013.

Spreier, S. W., Fontaine, M. H., and Malloy, R. L. "Leadership Run Amok: The Destructive Potential of Overachievers." *Harvard Business Review*, June 2006.

Spross, J. "How Bank of America Exposes the False Promise of the Shareholder Revolution." *Week*, October 1, 2015.

Sull, D., Homkes, R., and Sull, C. "Why Strategy Execution Unravels—and What to Do About It." *Harvard Business Review*, March 2015.

Sveen, L. "Do Tech Businesses See Workers as Disposable Assets?" *Denver Post*, April 29, 2016.

Swindall, C. *Engaged Leadership: Building a Culture to Overcome Employee Disengagement.* New York: John Wiley & Sons, 2007.

Tata, R., Hart, S. L., Sharma, A., and Sarkar, C. "Why Making Money Is Not Enough." *MITSloan Management Review*, June 18, 2013.

Thurm, S., and Lublin, J. S., "Peter Drucker's Legacy Includes Simple Advice: It's All About the People." *Wall Street Journal*, November 14, 2005.

Timberlake, C. "Four Seasons Adds Branded Luxury Jet to $119,000 Tours." BloombergBusiness, April 22, 2014.

Tischler, L. "IDEO's David Kelley on Design Thinking." *Fast Company*, February 1, 2009.

Tkaczyk, C. "How Google Works." *Fortune*, September 4, 2014.

de Tocqeville, A. *Democracy in America.* Translated and edited by H. C. Mansfield and D. Winthrop. Chicago: University of Chicago Press, 2002.

Treacy, M., and Wiersema, F. *The Discipline of Market Leaders.* Reading, MA: Addison-Wesley Publishing Company, 1995.

Trevail, C. "It's Time to Rethink the Chief Customer Officer Role." *Advertising Age*, March 17, 2016.

Vaillant, G. E. *Adaptation to Life.* Cambridge, MA: Harvard University Press, 1995.

van den Hurk, A. M. "In the New Year, Small Business Should Focus on the Customer." *Lexington Herald Leader*, December 27, 2015.

Vara, V. "The Push Against Performance Reviews." *New Yorker*, July 24, 2015.

Voigt, K. "Mergers Fail More Often than Marriages." CNN.com, May 22, 2009.

Von Drehle, D. "Encounters with the Arch-Genius." *Time*, March 7, 2016.

Wall Street Journal staff. "The Top Issues CEOs Face These Days." *Wall Street Journal* online, March 19, 2014.

Wapshott, N. *Keynes Hayek: The Clash That Defined Modern Economics.* New York: W. W. Norton and Company, 2011.

Watzlawick, P., Helmick Beavin, J., Jackson, D. *Pragmatics of Human Communication: A Study of Interactional Patterns, Pathologies and Paradoxes.* New York: W. W. Norton & Company, 1967.

Watzlawick, P., Weakland, J., and Fisch, R. *Change: Principles of Problem Formation and Problem Resolution.* New York: W. W. Norton & Company, 1974.

Welch, J., and Welch, S. "So Many Leaders Get This Wrong." LinkedIn.com, March 24, 2014.

Wheatley, M. *Finding Our Way: Leadership for an Uncertain Time.* San Francisco: Berrett-Koehler Publishers, Annotated ed., 2007.

Wheatley, M. J., and Kellner-Rogers, M. *A Simpler Way.* San Francisco: Berrett-Koehler Publishers, 1996.

Wiener, N. *Cybernetics.* Cambridge, MA: MIT Press, 1961.

Williams, R. *Culture.* London: Fontana, 1981.

Wolfe, N. *The Living Organization: Transforming Business to Create Extraordinary Results.* Irvine, CA: Quantum Leaders Publishing, 2011.

Zetlin, M. "Do You Understand Your Company's Personality?" *Computerworld,* March 10, 2014.

INDEX